Then and Now

Heine's Death Mask

W.D. JACKSON

Then and Now

Words in the Dark

MENARD PRESS
IN ASSOCIATION WITH
MPT BOOKS
2002

ISBN 1 874320 04 7

Menard Press
8 The Oaks, Woodside Avenue
London N12 8AR, UK
telephone and fax 020 8446 5571

MPT Books
School of Humanities
King's College London

Typeset by W.M. Pank,
Humanities Research Centres, King's College London
Printed by Alden Press, Oxford

World Wide Distribution and Representation (except North America)
Central Books / Troika
99 Wallis Road, Hackney Wick, London E9 5LN
telephone 020 8986 4854
fax 020 8533 5821

Distribution in North America
Small Press Distribution Inc.
1341 Seventh Street, Berkeley, CA 94710, USA

Rose, oh pure contradiction, desire
To be no one's sleep under so many
Eyelids.

Rilke

Contents

AUTHOR'S PROLOGUE

Events are our masters

Pascal

*

The words of a dead man
Are modified in the guts of the living

Auden

*

The world is the signature of the word

Heine

Reader, no matter where or when
The events which rule our lives occurred,
This book can only live again
If you choose to let each silent word
Resound here now in rhythm and rhyme.
In any place, at any time
We take our choices. Or they are
Taken not *by* but *for* us. We
Are the victims – or not – of history:
Of parents and family, *shouldn't* or *should*;
Of Jehovah – Jesus; Evil – Good;
Poverty – wealth; of political war
Or politic peace. From the sublime
To all the sick, ridiculous
Jokes chance happens to play on us:
Our loves, our hates, the social mores
Which tell us how to live our stories –
Tell us, in 1997,
Now God's no longer in his Heaven,
And we only live once – so 'Self's the Man' –
To get rich quick, or grab what we can –
To kick, bite, trample, arse-lick, run
Faster and faster, since winning's fun –
Though then remains forever ahead,
As well as behind. This blind, reductive
Race to the land of milk and honey,
This bright idea of the living dead –
'The more, the better' – more power, more money,
Possessions, pleasure – ignores how *enough*

Is choked and poisoned by *too much*,
As murder is always self-destructive,
Or clenched flesh dies in its own clutch.
But we live here, no matter where
Events have taken / will take place;
And we live now, no matter when
We fell – or did not fall – from grace.
At another time in another place
The family – tribe – caste – village grew
Like a tree whose roots and branches knew
Of light and dark and the changing seasons
But had no need of abstract reasons,
Unlike this glossy machine-age, cursed
And crazed with the need to justify –
Allure with carrot – threaten with stick:
We make ourselves – and others – and, worst,
The very world we live in – sick!
But we all join in – act or react
In fear or anger. How to remain
Human – or even not inhumane –
At such a time in such a place,
Is my only theme that matters. How
To release from the bloodless there of then
The here – the power – the peace of now
Is the entire responsibility,
Burden and opportunity –
Absurd – obscure – frightening – free –
Of each small soul. To let oneself be,
To go one's way, re-dream one's dream,
Creating the values time-tied men
Have destroyed or lost or merely lacked;
Also to choose one's style for each theme,
Whatever "the age demands" – is to set
The teeth of the age on edge. This set
Of pieces – these first words on the way

In search of peace amid the strife
Which "this strange disease of modern life"
Afflicts our world with – try to get
A mind's-eye view of what's gone wrong.
Reader, it's never *all* in the mind,
But since art's what we make of what we find,
And since we also see what we say,
I've tried to make these fragments fit
Into a pattern – hardly a song.
I wonder what you'll make of it,
As we make or 'read' our world – translate
Its sounds and signals. Life-artists let
Live and let flow, let the outer grow
Into an inner, imagined thing –
Transformed, not falsified. And yet
The world remains beyond us. Although
We may choose how we see, the thing we see
Is an image – no more – of reality.
And though there's more to come – of my life,
And of the work, that husband-and-wife
Duet – no human being can know
What horror or beauty events may bring
Over the hill or round the next bend.
Or where and when the way will end.

(1997/2001)

PART ONE
Self-Portrait as a White-Collar Worker (1):
From Hand to Mouth

1. DIFFICULTIES OF A
WHITE-COLLAR WORKER

"You appear, like me, to lead a very exhausting life, with the leisure
that you want always a mirage ahead of you, your holidays always
disturbed by foreseen (or unforeseen) calamities . . . What I do –
I am dealing alone with all the debts and claims of the bank under
the various Peace Treaties – sometimes takes a good deal of thought
and strength . . . The chief drawback to my present mode of life is
the lack of continuous time, not getting more than a few hours
together for myself, which breaks the concentration required for
getting out a poem of any length."

T.S. Eliot to John Quinn, 9 May 1921

WRITE what shall I write?
Who have sold my mind – into legal employment
By an electronic communications multinational
Having its headquarters in the Federal Republic of Germany
And offices, factories and subsidiaries in:

> 28 countries of Africa
> 24 countries of North and South America
> 32 countries of Asia and Australasia

and

> 26 countries – including 31 locations in Britain
> alone – of Western and Eastern Europe.

Write write what shall I write? Whose father,
Arthur Edward Cyril Parker, was appointed telephone operator
In the London offices of Faber & Gwyer, publishers,
At approximately the time that Mr Eliot joined the company
At a salary (my father

Not Mr Eliot) of one pound ten a week
Rising, by annual increments of five shillings –
Mr Eliot was a stickler when it came to figures –
To two pounds ten a week; with a bonus of thirty shillings
                    at Christmas
And one week's leave a year.

Here is a row of writing desks, orderly files, all looking
                    remarkably multinational,
Remarkably like each other, lit up by a neon flare
Of energy inexhaustibly supplied
By I cannot tell how many miracles of technology.
What shall I write? As one of so many
Crowding the way. As the long-lost son
Of one of the low,
Of one of the least of a statesman's difficulties,
Who fathered six children and later returned to Liverpool –
Or Bradford – or even stayed where he was in London –
And raised his children in another statesman's difficulty
Long overdue for clearance down by the river.

Father father (not among these necks
All correctly attired)
I a tired head
Among these heads
Who said right out loud, crumpets
In church on Easter Sunday,
Who threw away that sausage.
Father

As a difficult child
I was naturally subjected
To fourteen years of schooling, and learned
That one does things in order. For example,
One learns things in order

To pass exams and/or become employed
Which is what one lives in order
To do. So I laboriously studied
German – or Law – or Physics – or Engineering –
Or even Business Administration –
At the state's expense. After which I was appointed
At exactly what salary I have never been able to calculate
To the ranks of our company's myriad-minded
                        middle-management
And my thoughts were no longer free
Of charge. Languages
Have always been highly saleable on the job-market
Like muscle on a slave. How should I write
Understanding so little
I a tired head among these heads
Understanding so little –
Late evenings
And one month's leave a year
To relieve my mind
Of the boredom and fear
Which oppress and upset it.
"Fool," said my boss to me: "Poetry's a mug's
Game. Forget it."

Afterthought

"Or, if you really must, why not choose something great
And preferably entertaining –
Look in your bank-book
And write! – to translate?"

2. HEINRICH HEINE: *DEUTSCHLAND. EIN WINTERMÄRCHEN* (ll. 1-48)

November it was. And the cloudy skies
Grew daily more down-hearted;
The wind tore at the leaves on the trees;
And off for home I started.

And as I came to German soil
My heart seemed to be drumming
Harder and faster. In fact I think
The tears had started coming.

And when I heard my native tongue
I felt so strange for a minute
I thought my blissfully bleeding heart
Would spill all that was in it.

A girl was singing to a harp.
She sang with warm emotion
And tuneless voice, but I felt played
Upon by her devotion.

She sang of love and the pain of love,
Self-sacrifice, re-union
Above the clouds in that better world
Of unsuffering communion.

She sang of this earthly vale of tears,
Of the joys we cannot capture,
Of the life to come where the soul shall feast
In eternal radiant rapture.

She sang the old Forbearance Song,
The Lullaby of Later,
Which keeps the whining lumpen poor
From turning agitator.

I know the method, I know the text,
And I know the likes of the author;
I know that they secretly tipple wine
While openly preaching water.

A new song, a better song,
Companions, I shall write you!
And here and now on earth we'll build
A heaven to requite you.

We want our happiness here and now
On earth: we don't want hunger.
Let lazy bellies squander the thrift
Of hard-working hands no longer!

For human kind down here below
The bread we produce is ample –
And roses and myrtles, beauty and lust,
And garden peas, for example.

Yes, garden peas for everyone!
Come pile up the pods on the barrows.
And leave the heavenly pastures to
God's angels and the sparrows.

3. FROM HAND TO MOUTH.
OR: SNOWED UNDER
(Partly adapted from poems by Ernst Jandl)

"ob die abgebrochene hälfte
immer mit der bestrichenen seite
zu boden fallen müsse

stets mit unlust
betätige er
den kleinen handbesen

derlei trivialitäten
stießen
an den kern seiner existenz!"

Jandl, *Aus der Fremde*

i

Like dawn in the sky,
Cold splattered orts

Of egg and ketchup
Streak his blue plate.

ii

Give –

Since quite so much bread
Seems destined to fall
With the jam–side down

– him this day his sanity!

iii

With her eyes half-closed
In contentment the cat –

Cosy in her kitchen –
Ignores his ape-like mien.

iv

He slithers on icy pavements
Past fruitless gardens.

Pegged out washing creaks
On the biting wind.

v

A constipation of cars,
With and without passengers,

For minutes on end
Obstructs his progress.

vi

Old women cross his path.
One slips and drops her shopping.

Blood squirts on the dirty snow
From the flesh of an orange.

vii

The butterflies being sick
On his windy corners

Can neither stop nor
Go on. He goes on.

viii

There's a lot he could say
About the work in their office:

They educate managers:
He could dish up a course.

ix

Stapled to uniformity
8 hrs per day,

His mind becomes a depot
For files, punches, clips.

x

Discreetly policed
By rules and regimentations

His thoughts, like frightened citizens,
Conform or leave the country.

xi

By pylons, cables, wires
And switching systems

The secrets of the earth
Shall be netted like fish!

xii

Bangers and mash
With trifle for pudding

Reassure him at lunch
Of the delusions of childhood.

xiii

He eyes the ductile breasts
And tumid ankles

Of the complaisant bar-maid.
How platinum blonde her hair.

xiv

He keeps on meeting
People he doesn't know,

Though they mostly remain
Indigestible.

xv

In the tasteless poppet-chain
Of heads up arse-holes

It's where you spread the butter
That takes the cake.

xvi

2 jars of speeding wallop
Are pursued by cops of cuffee

Down the one-way street past his heart
Into the dead-end street of his heartburn.

xvii

The telephone demands
An incisive answer –

Incide and answer!
Outside a dancer.

xviii

His day gets longer
And longer.
           Or let's say
Shorter and shorter:

It doesn't stretch.

xix

Some people never flip
Their lids. They think that light

And reft have never been
Muxed ip.

Coda

He'd like to be Bad (or Good)
But worries about his liver.

Outside in the snowy wood
Each tree's a careless survivor.

He envies the wren in the wood
And the eel in the depths of the river.

4. HEINE: *DEUTSCHLAND.* *EIN WINTERMÄRCHEN* (ll. 77-120)

And while the maiden twittered and played
And panted after election,
The Prussian Customs Police undid
My bags for an inspection:

They poked their nose into trousers and shirts
And hankies, and fumbled for hidden
Laces and knick-knacks. And for books
Whose Knowledge was Forbidden.

O blockheads! poking in my bags,
Hoping to spot a dickey:
Confiscating the contraband
Of the mind's a bit more tricky!

There I have needlework finer than
Any of Brussels or Mechlin,
And once I've got my needles out
You won't hear yourselves for heckling.

And I carry knick-knacks in my head,
Jewels to crown and enthrone one,
The holy gems of a future God,
Of the great, as yet Unknown One.

And in my head there are many books.
Or, more plainly stated,
My head's a singing nest of the sort
You'd like to see confiscated.

Believe me, in Satan's reading-room
There can't be books more stinging:
They're twice as dicey as Hoffmann von F.'s
Unpolitical singing!

– A fellow-traveller starts to praise
But somehow in me arouses
Even more distrust of the Prussian State's
Long chain of customs-houses.

"This customs-union," he explains,
"Will characterize our nation –
Will help our divided Fatherland
To full Unification.

"It regulates each outward
Or material undertaking;
Whereas our spiritual unity
Is of the Censor's making.

"He regulates each inward
Aberrance, guiding sinners.
A United Germany we need –
Without us and within us."

5. THE MORE THE BETTER

Twelve televisions, bought not rented,
Deliver the News in two straight lines
To the lounge of the magnate who invented
The bead which lights up traffic signs.

His mates in flat caps find it funny,
Though some of them think it's going too far;
And yet it shows again how it's money
Makes living standards what they are.

And Hockneys, Caulfields, Joneses, etc.
Are stashed away under lock and key.
He considers, supping champagne, how to better a
Life of increasing ennui.

Now that they could afford to have children,
His wife's all grumble and no grunt.
The way she goes on at him 's bewilderin' –
What more does she bloody well want?

She's got her car, she's got her kitchen.
Kids just grow up and go away:
So what's the point? Her permanent bitching
Has turned him prematurely grey –

Like a cat, she says, in the dark. She goes
To a Writers' Workshop. Mills & Boon
Have accepted a 'formula' romance. Who knows,
She might be rich in her own right soon.

She can't stand swots or stuck-up pseudos
Who reckon art's for the sake of art
Or refers to itself (or something). Kudos
And royalties fire her simple heart.

Poetry's a mug's game. Some believers
In taking, though, grow tired of things
And take their lives – as though crying "Relieve us
Of trying to fly with unclean wings!"

So hundreds of Jesus-freak fanatics
Die for an ex-champ boxer who
Owned 18 Rolls Royce automatics
Till Jesus told him what to do.

And after her 22nd novel –
And 13 million sold – the wife
Went mad and withdrew to a disused hovel
In their mansion's grounds. Her burnt-out life

Was prolonged by drugs and private nurses.
Her husband had her certified;
Re-married and, despite her curses,
Was blessed with sons before he died.

6. THE GIFT OF TONGUES

The baby dreams in her dim bed
Like a warm fruit on a summer night,
As plump and full as if she'd fed
On prelapsarian liquid light;
She rocks on a dumb umbilical tree –
Or so I think of her as we

Relax of a Sunday afternoon,
Listening to music while howling snow
Is hurled outside our window. Soon
The spring will come. But now we go
Lying enarmed, enlegged together
Beyond the wordless rage of the weather –

And beyond the raging words of a world
Where minds are bought and sold to their harm,
Where men and bits of paper are hurled
In a windless, eyeless, endless storm,
Which cannot give, which thinks it can take,
Which can only undo, uproot, unmake

The fragile fruit of infancy,
Till the cold woman and loud-mouthed man
Can only grow in innocency
By luck or some well- or ill-laid plan . . .
My blood feels crumpled, cold, but your hand
Coaxes it quietly to a stand . . .

I have been suffering all this week
From a tongue gone brittle earning its bread
By chopping words. Your curious lick
Raises me from the clattering dead,
But your back's still tense. Our silent sex
Fits my concave to your convex

Which I gently stroke and warm with my palms
Till, moving down beneath the covers
I feel you slowly soften. My arms
Encircle flesh which only lovers –
Giving and taking with opening holes –
Soothe with their tongues and tongue with their souls.

7. INTIMATIONS OF MORTALITY FROM RECOLLECTIONS OF A RECENT HOLIDAY

While its well–off owners still think of us as friends,
    We've wangled a winter holiday together
In a high old farmhouse near where Austria ends
    In Czech barbed wire and ragged Asian weather,

And it reminds me of reading Wordsworth as a youth
    "In the great City pent". For now we're free
And the earth is all before us. Here where truth
    May "wake to perish never", here in the lee

    Of massive stones stacked low against the cold,
Where Bohemian winds can blue your baby's face –
Where it's "three seasons winter and one season cold" –
    Which suffer the placid soul to take its place

    Amid spectacular Scandinavian birds
    Awaiting the Northern summer. The herds
Of milch cows quietly, warmly shelter
From the wind whose ice-needles pelter

    The woman climbing the snowy slope.
The blue-faced child in her rucksack regards
A landscape gunned by border guards.
    All love, all hope

    Travel incognito at this border.
The woman brings schnapps, smoked ham and bread
    To our strong stone house – in order

To defend our souls (half-bled
        Of belief) from the colour of cold.

But the bullfinches' wind is red,
        And the eagles' gold.

(1985)

8. A GERMAN CHILDHOOD.
OR: FORMS AND FORCES

"History, Stephen said, is a nightmare from which I am trying to awake."
> **Ulysses**

Her charming manner on the telephone
And her orderly rows of files at the office
At first seem worlds away from where she learned
That a woman's better on her own,
That whatever praise she's earned –
Though she's no longer beaten or burned –
She necessarily suffers.

Our German secretary. Her Nazi father,
She informed my embarrassed wife and me
One evening after wurst and kraut,
Had relished public beatings. Rather
Than watch the prisoners shuffle out
To the crowd's indifferent shout
She'd help to make the official tea.

But being his eldest child meant she was forced
Whenever the Russian war demanded men
To present glum officers with her bouquet
And salute them goose-stepping off. The worst
Was when her father ran away –
Which taught her, she thinks, one meaning of "betray" –
And her mother refused to mention him again.

And now she has a flat all of her own.
Divorced after twenty years of domestic strife,
Her husband cuts her dead. Three grown-up boys
Are conscientious visitors. Alone,
She makes the most of "little joys".
Though she seems to think that hope somehow destroys
She did her duty as a mother, less as wife,

As her mother did before her. When the enemy
Threatened her birth-place with annihilation,
They stayed until the approaching dead
Din of Russian artillery
Forced them to flee. They fled
From danger behind towards danger ahead
In a crawling train without a destination.

Their carriage was an open cattle truck.
So the five children and their stubborn mother
Set off into the cold. At night the rain
Recalls their unrelenting lack of luck:
Afraid, humiliated, trapped again
On that freezing, overcrowded, half-starved train,
She dreams of how they sheltered one another.

Or she wakes pursued by nightmares of disgust
At potatoes dug with fingers out of the mud
Boiled in the baby's potty. And was
It the soldiers' guns or their lust
Which made her scream? So unquietly has
That rape been buried by what is
That what she will still cries for what she would

Do if she could – or would have done – till she
Declares us "mad" to want a second child:
Her English husband stood up for his rights,
But surely with the pill a woman's free . . .
She hints at the hopeless bondage of those nights,
Of three small children, at the bitter fights
And feeling (for the children's sake) defiled.

She seems to think that artists too are free
And, oddly, homosexuals. Those who bend
Events to their non-conformist will,
Or do so as far as she can see,
Give her some inner thrill.
She talks from inside herself until
I wonder has she ever had a friend,

If in the office human distances
Don't suit her better – getting machines to do
Without much trouble most of what she wants,
Typing dictations, making xeroxes –
Far from her children's cries and husband's grunts;
Where discipline is tough . . .
                                        But who confronts
Such choices, made without much meaning to?

And how much is chosen for us? How can one life
Awake from history's forms and hidden forces?
Each thinks he's different. Aren't we the same?
This woman, I, her husband, my wife –
Why do we emulate, praise, or blame?
What's in a person – a poem – a name?
Who runs our lives? or sets their future courses?

And what right have I – who hardly know
What I want from what I don't want any longer,
Who sell my mind in the same bright place,
Unwilling either to stay or go –
To analyse *her* tied-up case,
(Ignoring the beauty of her face):
Am I more hopeful? freer? stronger?

PART TWO

Heinrich Heine: Lyrisches Intermezzo
(Words and Screams)

1. ADAM DER ERSTE

"You sent your policeman down from Heaven
With his sword of flame to bust us,
And harassed us out of Paradise
Without pity, without justice!

"We're outlawed from our native land,
But we shan't regret our marriage.
You can't change the fact that I've enjoyed
The fruit of the Tree of Knowledge.

"And you can't change the fact that now I know
How small you are, a zero,
Though with death and thunder you bang about
Like some universal Nero.

"O God! how pitiful is this
Consilium abeundi!
You're what I call a Magnificus
Of the world, a Lumen Mundi!

"I for one shan't miss at all
The open fields of Eden:
It wasn't a proper Paradise –
It had trees which were Forbidden.

"I demand my rights, my Liberty!
If I find the least restriction,
For me your Paradise becomes
Imprisonment, affliction."

2. ALTES KAMINSTÜCK

Out-of-doors white flakes are blowing
Through the night; the storm is loud;
But the kitchen fire is glowing
Far from any town or crowd.

By the crackling fire I settle
Warm and dry in my favourite chair,
Lost in thought; the boiling kettle
Hums a long-forgotten air.

And a little cat sits playing,
Warms her paws beside the fire;
And the fire-light's weaving, swaying,
Fills my heart with strange desire.

Many a long-forgotten winter
Dawns and rises up again,
Bringing coloured mask and mummer,
Bringing vanished gentlemen.

Lovely women's knowing glances
Beckon enigmatically;
Harlequin cavorts and prances,
Laughing with unruly glee.

Farther off great gods of marble
Greet us; near them flowers grow
Dreamily, as in a fable;
Moonlit leaves wave to and fro.

Many a magic castle, gliding
Waterily, wobbles by;
Knights-at-arms come palely riding,
Leading page and pageantry.

But these visions fade forever,
Over-hasty, fast as dreams. –
Now the kettle's boiling over –
And the scalded kitten screams!

3. UNTERGANG DER SONNE

The beautiful sun
Has gone down peacefully into the sea;
And at once the surging waters are coloured
With the darkness of night:
Only the glow of evening
Still scatters them with golden shimmerings,
And the roaring power of the tide
Pushes white-topped waves up the beaches
Where they hurriedly jump for joy
Like a flock of woolly lambs
Driven by a singing shepherd-boy
Home of an evening.

"How beautiful the sun is!"
Said my friend after a long silence
As we continued along the beach;
And half-jokingly but half in earnest
He assured me that the sun was really
A beautiful woman who'd married
The sea-god out of convenience.
In the daytime she sauntered happily
Across the heavens, dressed up in scarlet
Or flashing her diamonds,
Universally loved and admired
By all creatures on earth
And gladdening all creatures on earth
With the warmth and light of her glances;
But every evening she was peevishly forced
To return once more

Into the wet house and barren arms
Of her senile husband.

"Believe me," my friend continued,
And he laughed – then sighed – then laughed again,
"They're really happily married down there!
When they're not asleep they're squabbling so fiercely
That the sea becomes rough on the surface
And sailors can hear in its roaring
The old man scolding his wife:
'You great gaudy eyesore! You
Cosmic courtesan!
All day you're hot for others
But at night, for me, you're cold and tired!'
Well, after a telling-off like that,
What else should the proud sun do
But burst into tears and complain of her misery
So long and so wretchedly that the sea-god
Leaps suddenly out of bed in desperation
And swims up quickly to the surface
To recover his breath and his bearings.

"And that's how I saw him yesterday evening,
Sticking up out of the sea as far as his chest.
He was wearing a jacket of yellow flannel
And a lily-white nightcap –
And had a shrivelled face."

4. GÖTTERDÄMMERUNG

"Who are these hooded hordes swarming
Over endless plains, stumbling in cracked earth
Ringed by the flat horizon only?"
The Waste Land

The 1st of May comes in with golden lights,
And with a silken gale and scents to inhale,
And tempts us like a friend with snowy blossoms
And greets us out of the eyes of a thousand violets
And rolls a fresh green flowery carpet out,
Woven with sunshine and with morning dewdrops,
And calls together all dear human creatures.
The mindless masses do as they're told at once.
The menfolk get their nankeen trousers on
And their Sunday coats with golden, shiny buttons;
The women dress themselves in virgin white;
Young hopefuls curl or clip their spring moustaches;
Young wenches let their bosoms bubble over;
The local poet puts his pen and paper
And glasses in his pocket; – and off they ramble,
The merry milling mob, out through the gates
And deposit themselves outside on the green grass,
Where all admire the industrious trees' new leafage,
Play with sweet little pastel-coloured flowers,
Listen to sweet little merrily-singing birds
And revel beneath the big blue tent of heaven.

May also came to me. She knocked three times
On the door and shouted, "It's me, the May,
You grey-faced dreamer! Come out and give me a kiss."
But I kept my door double-bolted, and answered

"You shan't tempt me, you snake in the grass.
I've seen through you and I've seen through
The ways of this world; have seen too much,
And much too deep – till all the joy's gone out of it
And anger and sickness wrestle in my heart.
I see straight through the stony, callous shells
Of human house and heart, and see the lies
And self-deceiving torment. Condemned
To read the ugly thoughts behind the virtuous
Faces, I see in this modest girl's shy blush
A ruthless hussy greedy with desire,
On that young virile fellow's eager skull
The gaudy cap and bells of a cheated fool!
And all I can see on earth are travesties
And ailing shadows: and how am I to know
If what we're building's a mad-house or a hospital?
I see through the foundations of the old
World as if they were crystal, and see the horror
Which May with all her merry foliage
Keeps trying to cover up. I see the dead
Laid out down there in narrow coffins
With their hands folded and their eyelids open,
With shrouds as white as their dead-white faces
And yellow worms that burrow through their lips.
I see the son sit down beside his mistress
For the fun of it upon his father's grave;
Around them nightingales sing bitter songs,
And the gentle meadow-flowers' malignant laughter
Sniggers until the dead man turns in his grave
And our old mother, the earth, shudders with pain."

Old earth! I feel you suffer when I see
The red fire burning deep inside your bosom –
And see a thousand veins begin to bleed;
I ache as your old scars split again, burst open

And flame and smoking blood stream wildly out of them!
I see your ancient rock-ribbed brood of sons –
Their huge forms clambering from the dark abyss
Wielding red torches in their barbarous hands; –
They prop their iron ladders up against heaven
Wildly attacking God's citadel; – and dwarfs,
Black ones, climb after them; – and with a crackle
The silver stars of heaven turn into dust;
The golden curtain of God's tent is torn
By impudent hands; and howling hosts of innocent
Angels get thrown down roughly on their faces.
God's face turns livid: he clutches his throne,
Snatches the crown from his head, rips out his hair –
And the unruly rabble crowd up closer and closer.
The giants catapult their flaming torches
Far and wide into heaven; the dwarfs let fly
With flaming whips across angelic backs
Till the angels struggle and writhe in agony –
Get swung around and slung out by the hair.
And now I can see my own familiar angel,
With his golden curls, his lighted countenance,
With everlasting love about his lips,
And everlasting bliss in his blue eyes –
And a disgusting ugly black hobgoblin
Snatches him up off the ground, my pallid angel,
Ogles and mocks his other-worldly body,
Embraces him with a tender, firm embrace –
And a bellowing scream jars through the universe,
The columns fracture, earth and heaven tumble
And crash together, and the old night reigns.

5. "ES TRÄUMTE MIR VON EINER SOMMERNACHT"

I dreamt it was a moonlit summer-night,
And glorious works of architects and masons
Lay pale and weathered in the gleaming light,
Left over from the time of the Renaissance.

And here and there among the ruins rose
A lonely Doric capital and column,
Scanning the distant firmament, as though
To scorn its thunder: the effect was solemn.

While all about lay broken on the ground
Pieces of portal, statues out of gables –
Sphinx, centaur, satyr: chimeras which compound
The human with the bestial in old fables.

A lidless stone sarcophagus stood bared
Among the debris, quite unmutilated;
Inside the coffin, also unimpaired,
A gently suffering dead man lay and waited.

And caryatids seemed laboriously
To crane their chiselled necks to keep it mounted.
On one side and the other you could see,
In crowded bas-reliefs, old myths recounted:

The great Olympic gods, reigning in pride,
In slothful lust and ignorance of what sin is;
Adam and Eve, carved next to them, supplied
With chaste Judaic-Christian fig-leaf pinnies.

Paris and Helen, Hector and the Fall
Of Troy were there: the city's walls were flaming.
Moses and Aaron stood beneath the pall,
And Judith, Holofernes, Esther, Haman.

The god of love was likewise to be seen,
Phoebus Apollo, Vulcan, Lady Venus,
Pluto, Proserpina, and the Go-between,
Bacchus the god, Priapus and Silenus.

And next to them was Balaam's famous ass –
Bespeaking what the Holy Bible taught us –
Also the test which Abraham had to pass,
And Lot, besotted with his sinful daughters.

Here was Herodias' dance, performed so well
She claimed the Baptist's head – someone was even
Dishing it up! And Satan, sunk in Hell,
While Peter bore the mighty key of Heaven:

And, here, were represented one by one
The outrageous doings of Jove, the god of loinage,
Who seduced Leda as a lanky swan
And Danae as a shower of golden coinage.

Here you could see Diana's savage chase,
Her mastiffs and her nymphs with tucked-up dresses;
Huge Hercules making the spinning-wheel race,
His brawn half-hid in female flimsinesses:

And next to them Mt Sinai, veiled in cloud,
And on the mountain Israel with his oxen;
Young Jesus still in the temple, asking loud
Questions to try and trip the orthodox on.

These vivid oppositions paired and jarred:
The Greeks' unthinking joy / the strict theology
Of Judaism. And the ivy twined its hard
Tendrils round both in arabesque biology.

But as I dreamed that I stood musing on
These statues like a sort of poet / boffin,
It strangely dawned on me: I was the man
Who lay there dead inside that marble coffin.

And, stranger still, a most mysterious flower,
Whose violet, sulphur-yellow leaves molested
And charmed my senses with a savage power,
Bloomed darkly at the head of where I rested.

The 'passion-flower' I think I've heard it called
And Golgotha the place where it first sprouted
When Christ was crucified to save the world –
From ground on which his holy blood had spouted.

The flower bears witness to the blood, they say,
And carries in its cup what look like sketches
Of instruments of torture, tools which may
Be used for making martyrs out of wretches.

Yes, everything that anyone could hope
To see a Son of God be made to sample:
The crown of thorns, the cup, the scourge, the rope,
The cross, the nails, the hammer, for example.

And such a flower was bending over me
Where I lay dead, as silent as a woman
In mourning, kissing inconsolably
My corpse with all the kisses she could summon.

And in the magic of my dream the flower
Of sulphur-yellow passion, in the queerest
Imaginable way started to tower
Into a woman – into, yes, my dearest!

You were the flower, yes you, my darling child!
I recognized you from your tender kisses:
No flower's lips ever felt so soft, or wild –
No flower's tears ever burned like my young miss's!

My eyes were closed. Yet with the deeper sight
Which lovers have I saw your face before me,
Glimmering and blessed. In ghostly lunar light
You fixed your eyes on me – as if to draw me.

We didn't speak, and yet my heart perceived
The half-formed, secret thoughts you left unspoken.
The spoken word is shameless. Less deceived,
The purer flower of silence blooms unbroken.

A wordless dialogue! Strange though it seems,
The hours pass quickly in such silent chatter:
The loving small-talk of mid-summer dreams
Woven out of delightful / dreadful matter.

But never ask which matters we discussed! –
Ask the green grass what glow-worms say by glowing,
Ask rippling waves what secrets they entrust
To rivers. Ask the west wind what it's blowing.

Ask the carbuncle what it sparkles for,
Ask roses and night-violets what they smell of,
But never ask the moonlit Passion-flower
Or her dead friend what wordless looks can tell of.

I've no idea how long I dreamt I lay
Dreaming of joy in that cool coffin standing
Among the debris. But it melts away,
The peace that passes human understanding.

Only the stillness of the grave can give
Such ecstasy so purely beyond measure:
Our joys are crude and foolish while we live –
Our passions cramped, lusts without peace or pleasure.

Yes, even that state of bliss was driven away,
By noises from outside: stamping like cattle,
Two loud-mouthed crowds rushed into dusty fray.
My flower withdrew from that insane word-battle.

I heard a furious, loud, wrangling to-do:
A great debate arose. Nothing could save us.
I thought I recognized a voice or two
As coming from my basso relievos!

Could they *be haunted by such bigotry?*
Could marble phantoms really be disputing?
Moses' anathemas so savagely
Compete with Pan's wild shouts and pagan fluting?

The True will always fight the Beautiful:
Two human mobs perpetually at variance!
There'll never be an end to the great, dull,
Mud-slinging hubbub: Hellenes v. Barbarians.

They cursed, they swore! But none could finish off
The stale controversies, the same old squabbles;
Till Balaam's donkey's brays, like whooping-cough,
Out-shouted both divine and saintly rabbles.

Its nauseous sobbing hee-haws seemed to come
From my throat too: I felt them start to choke me!
At last, in desperation, struggling to stem
The ugly din, I shouted out – which woke me.

6. "WORTE! WORTE! KEINE TATEN!"

Words, words, words, and nothing doing!
Never flesh, my dear, my poppet! –
Never any dumplings stewing –
Always soul! No roast to top it!

But the horse of passion gallops
Pretty wildly – daily too –
And perhaps the solid wallops
Of the loins aren't good for you.

In that steeple-chase with Cupid,
Gentle child, in fact I fear
You might end up knocked half-stupid:
Love's a savage hunt, my dear.

Yes, I'd say your health demands
Lovers of my kind who linger
On and on with shrivelled glands,
Who can hardly raise a finger.

Therefore by all means unbosom
Till our hearts are hand in glove,
For your health will surely blossom
On such sanitary love.

PART THREE

Self-Portrait as a White-Collar Worker (2):
From Then to Now

1. THE PROGRESS OF TRUTH
(Written after Watching a TV Production of
Berthold Brecht's Life of Galileo)

"Doubt thou the stars are fire,
Doubt that the sun doth move,
Doubt truth to be a liar,
But never doubt I love.

O dear Ophelia, I am ill at these numbers. I have not art
to reckon my groans. But that I love thee best, O most
best, believe it. Adieu.
　　　　　Thine evermore, most dear lady, whilst this
　　　　　machine is to him,
　　　　　　　　　　　Hamlet." (1601)

After the heretical Galileo
Had ceased to believe his eyes

Other than with the unnatural aid
Of devilish tricky lenses,

Proposing Earth's inglorious progress
Around an unmoving sun –

A star like any other star
(No longer silver, gold), –

And abstract mechanical experimentation
Like a pirate's cannonball

Had probed the still, unprofitable spirit
Of scholastic introversion,

While Paul in his barren grave was busy
Blowing dogmatic raspberries

And blessing the Inquisition which
Was tweaking the unorthodox –

Unracked by doubt, unworried lest dogma
Had naturally nurtured Science

By paving a one-way highway to
The death of myth, the secession

Of outer worlds from inner ones –
It grew to irk more concrete minds,

Or minds less eager to ask how
Than why of mathematics,

Like Hamlet's, or John Donne's, who wrote
"The new Philosophy calls all in doubt;

"The Sun is lost, and th'earth, and no mans wit
Can well direct him where to looke for it",

That many a thing we cannot see
Is true; and many a thing

Which the mind has always thought it has seen
Is untrue: if what happens

Can be proved not to have happened, if
What doesn't happen can

Be proved to happen; if what is
Is not, and what is not

Is, why, o Galileo, and how –
Having tried our best to believe

That only what's capable of proof
May be believed (the rest

Is hypothetical) – are *we* "To be
Or not"? What *happened?* O

Now that our world has been relieved
Not merely of myth and magic

But, Mr Galileo, even
Of nicely explained religion,

Please use that 'normous brain and tell us
Where is our unity? –

O Mr Galileo, tell us
Exactly how to fasten

A bundle of loose hypotheses
About us in such a way

As to bandage the bleeding all–in–each
Or bind the dispersing soul

Into some vestige of unity.

2. PARADISE ISLAND

"Pleasure . . . generates submission."
Marcuse (1964)

The time goes by so quickly:
Already another week!

He sits on the terrace drinking
His wine, too heady to think

But knowing it must be Sunday
Since in families or one by one

Pale strangers arrive, replacing
Brown strangers who've left without trace.

A group gets out of a taxi –
And before they've even unpacked

Their brand-new bags, the children
Are off to the beach, half-wild

To cool themselves, abandoning
Their clothes on the burning sand.

He envies their innocent freedom,
Though here even *he* feels free

Enough to decide to follow:
The eternal breakers roll

Him up and down in their comfy
Bosoms. The raging sun

Is tamed by perfumed lotions
And stylish glasses, although

Some skins still burn severely.
But a tan is why they're here

And bulging middle-aged udders
And even grandmothers' dugs

Are all hung out. The youngest
Are crying now among

The sun-shades: the sand keeps scorching
Their feet. And swimmers lurch

Across it – plunge in the water
Abruptly. Wishing he'd brought

His novel and not Marcuse's
Abstrusities, he peruses

With imperfect understanding
Pages sprinkled with sand

On the imperfect understanding
Of *One-Dimensional Man*;

But the heat, he soon concludes,
Distracts one's attention. Who

Cares if he ever re-reads this
Anyway?! What he needs

Is something entertaining,
To help him recuperate,

Not academic abstraction –
Though turning to do his back

He observes their neighbours' daughter
Being pestered by three or four

Unacademic admirers.
The sun sets the blood on fire,

They say: the beach is blazing
With idyllically easy lays

And couples erotically sunning
Their zones. All harmless fun,

Of course, though so much raging
Sex makes him feel his age

And, leaving the beach to Beauty,
They take a taxi to view

A local monastery: religion
Is more relaxing. This fridge

Of a church though is gloomily cared for
By nuns who make it clear

That his wife's 'uncovered'. A farmer
Shows more respect. With the charm

Of some prehistoric Golden
Age, he courteously holds

His hat and beads, inclining
His grizzled head as a sign

That he knows of secret places.
With a smile on his honest face

He plucks her oregano
In bunches, leading them on

Between flowering oleander,
Olive-trees, vineyards, round

White houses down to a lakeside.
When they smile and she starts to take

His photo, he sticks his palm out
For drachmas. *Ah well, no harm*

In helping. He swiftly pockets
His pickings and scuttles back

To the church. The lake is shining,
A deeper blue than the sky,

Though its bushy shores are crowded
With tourists, some of them loud

And drunk. Still, here you see Nature
In an almost primal state:

Its unpolluted colours
Make even the ads look dull,

Which is also why they come here –
To get away from home,

Where they spend their week-days earning
The money they need to burn,

Though he feels that life's succeeding
When they get the things they need,

For instance another taxi
Which he summons to take them back

Along the beautiful coast-line
Unfortunately marred by the ghosts

Of unfinished abandoned buildings,
Like lives gone unfulfilled.

But now it's almost evening,
Almost time to eat

At the always friendly taverna
With its almost ethnic fare

Where nothing is ever a problem –
Not even thankless plebs

Objecting to soft tomatoes
In the salad. Sick at heart,

He's glad they'll soon be flying
Back to the grind. Asked why,

He'd probably answer "No comment" –
Even to himself. They'll zoom

In a tube of air-tight metal
Home through the sky, and get

Nostalgic, calmed by their dose of
Pleasure, their paradise

On earth, complaisantly waiting
For next year's holiday.

3. HEINRICH HEINE: *DAS SKLAVENSCHIFF*

i

The supercargo Mynheer van Koek
Sits in his cabin reviewing
The wholesale value of his load
And totting up the profit ensuing.

"The rubber's good, the pepper's good:
I've three hundred barrels and sackfuls.
There's stacks of ivory and bags of gold –
But what'll sell best's the poor black fools!

"Their flesh is firm, their sinews hard
As iron of the finest quality:
Six hundred dirt-cheap niggers of
Guaranteed pure Senegality!

"I swopped them for schnapps and baubles of steel
And beads for their chieftains to toff it in;
If half of them stay alive, I take
Eight hundred per cent profit in.

"If just three hundred stay alive
Till Rio de Janeiro,
I'm promised a hundred ducats a head
From the firm of Gonzales Perreiro."

Mynheer van Koek is torn from his thoughts
Abruptly: van der Smissen,
The good ship's doctor, steps inside
Advising him to listen.

"Well now, sea-surgeon," demands van Koek
Of this leanest of human figures,
Whose nose is full of blood-red warts:
"How are my darling niggers?"

The doctor thanks him for asking and says,
"Mynheer, we can overlook it
No longer: far too many of them
Are starting to kick the bucket.

"Two's been our average loss, but today
Seven joined the powers infernal –
Four men, three women. I've made a note
Of the death-rate in our journal.

"I inspected the corpses with great care:
These rascals have no notion
Of right or wrong – they'll pretend they're dead
Just to get thrown in the ocean.

"I removed the irons from those that were cold;
I change my habits rarely –
And dumped them as usual in the sea
This morning bright and early.

"At once there came shooting out of the waves
The sharks, a whole convention
Of connoisseurs of nigger-flesh;
I think of it as their pension.

"For ever since we left the coast,
Where the ship leads they follow;
The beasts smell out the corpses – and
Sniff – snap – gobble – swallow.

"It's fun to watch the way they snap
At the bodies, one or two angling
In at the head or leg. The rest
Gulp down the bits left dangling.

"And when breakfast's all gone they happily
Tumble around our planking; you
Would swear they were looking you straight in the eye –
Just as if they were thanking you!"

Van Koek breaks in on this fine speech
With a sigh. "How can I lessen
This evil? How can I prevent
Mortality's progression?"

The doctor answers, "A lot of the blacks
Have died of their own doing:
Their bad breath smells so foul that the air
Of the hold's not fit to spew in.

"And many have died depressed, been bored
To death by idle slacking.
A breath of air, music and dance –
And we'll soon send this sickness packing."

"What a splendid idea!" exclaims van Koek.
"My first-class nautical leecher
Is wiser than Aristotle, who
Was Alexander's teacher!

"In Delft the President of our
Society of Tulip-growers,
Though clever, isn't blessed with half
Of your commonsensical powers.

"Music! music! All blacks on deck!
Everyone hopping and skipping!
And if any black should fail to enjoy
Himself he gets a whipping."

ii

High in the firmament of heaven
A thousand stars are thronging:
Their large wise eyes look brightly down
Like a woman's filled with longing.

They gaze upon the sea which far
And wide lies covered over
With phosphorescent purple mist;
The wavelets lap like a lover.

Not a sail on the slave-ship flaps: it lies
As if it had lost its rigging;
But on deck the lanterns flare to the blare
Of a dance-band's jig-a-jig-jigging!

The helmsman scrapes a violin;
The boys fetch a tub and thump it;
The cook pipes up on his battered flute;
The doctor blows a trumpet.

A hundred negroes, men and women,
Are shouting for joy and stomping
Like mad in a circle. Clanking chains
Accompany their jumping.

They stamp the deck with furious glee,
And several black beauties, moaning
Lustily, clasp their naked men;
Though others are crying and groaning.

70

The gaoler is Maître des Plaisirs;
He whips all less than hearty
Dancers, driving them on to get
More pleasure from the party.

With a rum-tum-tum and fiddle-de-dee!
Up from the depths come nosing
Sea-monsters, woken by the din –
Some drunk with sleep, some dozing.

The dull-brained sharks come swimming up ·
Until there are several hundred
Staring nonplussed at the ship, where it looks
As though somebody must have blundered.

Perceiving it's not yet breakfast-time
They open their gullets, chawing
The air with yawns and displaying rows
Of teeth you could use for sawing.

With a rum-tum-tum and fiddle-de-dee –
There's no end to the celebration.
The sharks start biting their own tails
In ravenous frustration.

I don't think music moves them much,
Or other beasts which prey so.
"Let no such brute be trusted." Did
Not Albion's poet say so?

With a fiddle-de-dee and rum-tum-tum –
The celebration is endless.
Beside the foremast Mynheer van Koek
Prays to the Friend of the friendless:

"O Lord, for Jesus Christ's sake, spare
My blacks.   Should their heathen prattle
Enrage Thee, Lord, please don't forget
They're only foolish cattle.

"Spare them for Jesus' sake, who died
To save each wretched sinner!
For I need at least three hundred, Lord,
To make the trip a winner."

4. AT HOME AMONG STRANGERS

With time to kill between the exhibition
Of David Hockney's *Lonely Hearts' Club Band*
And the start of the play, preoccupied
By images of heroes – boyfriends – fairy-tales –
Elderly parents – C.P. Cavafy –
I make the unthinking mistake (or have I
Become a stranger where I was born?)
Of deciding to go on foot
From the principal tourist attraction
Of this run-down city – a monolithic dock,
The work of insane but fearless giants,
Now cluttered with boutiques and gift-shops
Selling trivia, postcards, confectionery –
Up through the centre of town
Towards the theatre. But
It's Sunday: the new pedestrian precinct,
Stretching into the distance
Like a surrealist vista,
Is deserted and litter-strewn; shut-up shops
And restaurants which might never have opened
Threaten my progress; a group of blacks
Are setting fire to a litter-basket
Outside a fast-food shop; a group of skin-heads
Abuse them obscenely, as I slink between,
Clutching my precious possessions. A police-car
Approaches slowly, like a cruising shark
Through polluted water; the small fry scatter;
And though I pretend I always stroll
Through the heart of the city on Sunday –
Through this cauterized gap in the city –

The police are suspicious: "To the *theatre?*"
I imagine them bawling
In disbelief. But at last I arrive,
Stifling a groan as I realize
This play is the sort of happening
In which you are invited / expected / compelled
To get up and do something. The principal actress,
Who has also developed
And now freely-and-easily improvises
The group-therapeutic text, is from New York.
She is moved to tears and raucous laughter
By her childhood memories. So
Is the audience. She unironically believes
In the sexual energy of go-go dancing
And in "democratic communication". So
Do we. She is bored by outmoded classics
Which always take place on stage, as though the actors –
Or any other artist ("they all think they're God") –
Were somehow different. And yet
So many, many friends
Have died of AIDS! She wonders
If we can imagine
What that has done
To her. The audience
Is obviously moved
By this moving woman – obviously relieved
By the thought of not being different
Or on its own. She then instructs us
To join in the dancing. The stage is filled
With a heaving mountain of people. The actress
Removes her clothes to show her sincerity:
Her full-blown body's past it – but why worry?
Everyone is happy and more than a few ecstatic.
The lights are bright and colourful;
The surrounding darkness is hardly visible.

She obviously loves us. We obviously love her –
Especially those who felt too shy
To get up and dance – including me,
Who have been thinking she might show us
How to walk unafraid through that precinct –
And when she falls off the stage by accident,
Bruising her buttock, a hundred hands
Are ready to help her.

5. THE PARK ON SUNDAY

"The poet and the dreamer are distinct . . .
The one pours out a balm upon the world,
The other vexes it."

– These crossed-out lines of Keats' keep running through
My troubled mind. The chestnuts overhead
Like forests painted on a Grecian urn
Have all the stillness that I need to learn:
"Ah, happy, happy boughs! that cannot shed
Your leaves, nor ever bid the Spring adieu . . ."

The parks where I grew up are not so quiet:
Sticks and stones flew thick again last night
And milk-bottles filled with petrol, fused with a rag,
Bombed local business. Mother's shopping bag
Was stuffed with loot. Through the smoky, rough-tongued light
An inner-city back-streets mob ran riot.

My birthplace. But not my daughter's. She plays amid flowers
In peacefulness and sunshine. Their scented beds
Are calmly contemplated by the birds
While I, in search of wordlessness not words,
Gaze at the park's grass-greens, rose-reds,
For such self-regarding hours

As others might take for loitering in a city
Where if you're young and haven't got a job
They frisk you publicly, abuse and treat you
Like a nigger; where you're scared they'd beat you

If you gave them a chance. School-children riot and rob
In a murderous struggle for revenge or pity,

And the country's leader at a county do
Where even her bodyguards wear bowler-hats
Drones in her phoney accent, "Whoever 'd've thought
Such things could happen in England?" Where she bought
Her get-up, she thinks, is England. High-rise flats
And derelict back-to-backs are England too –

And shopping streets where more than half the shops
Are boarded up, while the rest display poor wares;
And unsold houses, half-deserted pubs:
The unemployed in cut-price porno clubs
With no hope of work or money. The stripper bares
Her body only until the music stops.

– And yet who calls the tune? Who helps the schools
To bribe and bully children into thinking
That their aim in life is work, that work is done
For money, not love; life's no more fun
Than learning, but you might get stinking
Rich if you ply the bribe-and-bully rules?

"How right the workers are," George Orwell said,
"To put the belly before the soul
In point of time." But even if he
Was right in Wigan in 1933,
Now it's the soul that's starved. The police, the dole
Have goaded the neither ragged nor unfed

To an anxious and involuntary flailing
Whose highest motivation is the need
To be issued with regulation fetters
By those they *prefer* to regard as their betters

And with whom they share the easy creed
Which envies strength and blames the weak for failing!

– I stumble against a bench. My daughter plays
Far from the office or from book-shop shelves
Under the chestnut trees. But our favourite park
Appears less peaceful now – less light than dark,
Dark, dark. We blind ourselves, and maim ourselves,
By thinking too precisely on what pays,

On where we're aimed and how we're going,
Till our time-ridden world needs slowing, slowing.

Oh we love and hate what helps us keep
On scrambling up the nearest heap
Of material or ethereal gain –
Or stops us slithering down again!

Our movements lose the name of action –
Our satisfactions satisfaction –

But comfort's still comfort, success success,
And since to be is to possess
The more we've got or get the less
We resent the usual strain and stress:

And the dole's still the dole – humiliation,
Aggro, envy, bored frustration.

Forever struggling to make ends meet,
Forever under each other's feet –
While your older kids are on the street
And, learning to expect defeat,
Your younger kids lose hope at school –
Who wouldn't feel useless or a fool?

Fool! Though the undefeated fly
Beyond the park through the pathless sky
Or sing all Sunday afternoon
(But birdsong is never out of tune),

The word alone reminds me of
So much I'd prefer to be above
On this way of life I'm halfway through
But daily do or fail to do.

And failure's one way to explain
The boredom, the fear, the stress and strain –
Heart trouble – impotence – and cancers –
But we're too keen on one-word answers,

On knowledge as know-how, which we trade
For an aim in life – thus briskly evade
(If we can) bohemian conflicts of
What ought we to value, hate or love

Apart from clear-cut profits and losses –
And our immediate boss and his bosses!

Till even hard-and-fast succeeders,
Wine-bibbers, knowledgeable feeders,
Though steeped in the rites and joyless frolics
Of self-respecting workaholics,

Suffer from nameless discontentments –
Sleeplessness – ulcers – confused resentments
At bureaucratic tyranny,
Which binds you while it leaves you free –
Is everywhere and nowhere – can
Make/mar you by a change of plan –

Repay you with the threat of loss –
Or make a thug your boss.

– The Afghan prances proudly by
Which only last Sunday nipped my thigh.
The rosebeds' soil is hard and browned
But my daughter brings a worm she's found,
Which wriggles – as I suppose it must,
Once dropped there – in the sunny dust.

As a child I dreamt of how I'd like
To cycle away on a flying bike
Or be a fearless Peter Pan.
The child is father of the man –
What worked the sad Hook-hungry croc-
odile if not the swallowed clock? –
And now I rise from my swivel chair,
Fling files and memos everywhere
As if one could simply leave an office,
As if there were really better offers
Of lives elsewhere. But since there aren't
Or since at any rate we can't
As long as our own contribution
Helps self-perpetuate an institution
Whose masters are its slaves, we resign
Ourselves to falling in the line
Of duty, looting what we can
Since money is what makes the man –
Fiddling expenses, pinching paper,
In on any dodge or caper
That can be cut to fit the tune
We march or crawl to. Picaroon,
Tempted by ifs, in awe of buts,
Hating inferior colleagues' guts,

Who works to live, who lives to work?
We ought to admit we're in the dark!

But instead we keep on plugging away
Ambitiously from here and now
To imagined deadlines, praise or pay
In an unreal future, ignoring how

All action turns to flailing in
So far as it's bullied by time
And bribed by purpose. Petrol-bombs, skin-
Heads, looting sound at once like crime

But the force and lures we all deploy
To obtain what we've been schooled to desire
With quiet legality destroy
Our souls in the great industrial fire:

Fire-blinded and severely burned
Yet ever assured of better health
We gloat that folly and weakness earned
The blue-collar millionaire his wealth.

But we're lost in the back-streets. Recently I –
A stranger at home for years,
Informed by the media *where* and *why*
The mob ran riot – have felt goaded by fears
Of why and where my life is aimed,
Felt puzzled again, blinded, maimed.

– Words, *words* we need! The birds which contemplated
The flower-beds hop and scatter now, disturbed
By a loud-mouthed dog. Have I created –
Ever – a peace less curbed, less easily perturbed?

Even the park deceives in its wordless way:
Tomorrow's another working day. All day.

– A *riot* of words! A monstrous, mechanical donkey
Has deafened and hoofed our wordless working world
So long it looks lop-sided and runs wonky!
If it's not too late, if we haven't been hurled
So far off course there's no way back until
Our greeds and fears consume themselves. Meanwhile,

It seems that more than one individual
Is sick and tired of insult, feels like spitting
It back in someone's face – as petrol
Or poem. You might as well make shitting
Your aim in life as working for fear or money.
The policeman in the land of milk and honey

Is a measure of how we force our half-bled souls
To knuckle under; the rioters' angry stealing
Of how we lure them. As for other goals
We've long been robbed of words: trained thought,
                                    trained feeling,
Cripple our minds. But man is not a beast
And these street-running rioters cry to be released

From what they cannot think of as oppression
And therefore half-mistake for unemployment
And racist rozzers. A – Keatsian – verbal obsession
With art's unhurried, sure, unending enjoyment
Of seeing the world through freely contemplating
The self might thus be worth elucidating –

Though Keats himself might stutter in a place
Where thirty years ago even I once threw
A stone through a teacher's window. By the grace

82

Of Sunday School the old gradgrind never knew
That it was me – the prefect at the front
Who conned his lessons. An isolated stunt,

Which reminds me of the bomb-site where we'd played
At cops-and-robbers with stolen fire as a base
To jump through: daring it, flushed and afraid
We'd be caught and punished. Now, as on Guy Fawkes' Days,
The fires are bigger. But still of the same sort.
– If only we could steal back words, steal thought,

Or liberate thought in a riot of words
For each to defend himself as best he can
Against the strait-laced bureaucratic turds
Which'd bed men down in a travesty of man –
A thoughtless, loveless, bribed, tired, bullied brute
In an overall, a uniform, or suit!

Postscript

"Ten red ones," my daughter says. At the age of two,
As she learns to see more clearly how things are
She learns to name them. The roses are "red", not "blue".
But the imagination rarely gets that far! –
Perceiving and performing what's been taught us,
We behave like mobs of world- and word-distorters.

Yet every child sees Paradise before
It's kicked in the head by that mad donkey. Later
"Beauty is Truth, Truth Beauty" is a saw
Meaningless to most of us. But its creator
Knew it might change the world. And if "might" 's not much,
Suffer the little children, for of such

Is faith, hope, love. Like lilies of the field
The children take no thought for the things of the morrow.
But wounds in the mind are only slowly healed
And, wounded, a thing of beauty's dark with sorrow.
My daughter brings a broken rose she's found.
But the chestnuts' roots grope deep in the dark ground.

(1981/1987-88)

6. WORDS IN THE DARK

They've all gone home. Across the road
   The office lights flick quietly out
As Friday evening lightens the load
   On all our minds. The latest bout
With time is over. Time has slowed.
   Yet boss and secretary must
Still push through patient traffic-jams
   Where car-horns, exhaust fumes and dust
Tire harassed mothers pushing prams
   With infants who can only trust
That what gets done to them is right,
   Or not too wrong, and not a joke.
Striking a momentary light,
   I blow a cloud of heat and smoke
In the rough direction of the night.
   Four storeys down the lights of cars
Follow-my-leader through the dusk,
   As soldiers still embark for wars –
Or all good students wore subfusc –
   Or punk kids follow their punk stars.
All do what everybody does.
   I pay my bills – don't stretch my wings –
We're here because we're here because
   We're good at putting up with things.
And life feels like it always *was*
   The human race heroically
But blindly doing as it's told:
   Which must be what I cannot see

At our window – as when, five-years-old,
    Our school-class stood excitedly
With thousands lining the road between
    The airport and more important places
In that run-down city to see the Queen
    Who, travelling on to see the races,
Blessed us from her limousine . . .
    With laughter, aching legs and tears,
Waving one hand, one shoulder touching,
    For what seemed hours we practised cheers
In rows by height, like soldiers, clutching
    Blue New Testament souvenirs.
Across that road I might have seen
    Up a narrow, evil-smelling jigger
With crumbling walls one place the Queen
    Would stop. O cathedral! better, bigger
Than either playground or canteen –
    Provided you were good. Or tried
To be as good as worthless sinners –
    Worthy of punishment for pride
And the greeds and sloth deep down within us –
    Could be on that blackened riverside.
More sherbet, liquorice, plastic toys,
    I thought, rewarded the good as gold
"Above" than in Santa's grotto! "Joys
    Await you there. Here all grows old,
Then dies. Be prudent, girls and boys,
    And

            'Lay up treasure in Heaven!
            Life will pass away.
            Lay up treasure in abundant measure
            For the great Accounting Day.
            Lay up treasure in Heaven!
            Though men shall be poor,
            Thou shalt reign with the Son of God

For evermore.' "
Minds moulded by "the old, old story
    Of unseen things above,
    Of Jesus and His Glory,
    Of Jesus and His Love",
  Driven on by welcome punishment,
Our lives seem spent on Purgatory –
    "Tell me the old, old story
    As to a little child,
    For I am weak and weary
    And tempted and beguiled":
  That sin-heap from the Fundament
Of Man 's a fertile promontory,
  We think, from which like twinkling planes
Those blessed with ultimate success
  Take off. Their fame, which never wanes,
Dazzles us. Failing to progress,
  We fret – and take still greater pains,
As if choirs of ecstatic businessmen
  And millionaires in flashy ties,
Exalted by their acumen,
  Sang down to us from some Paradise
Of stars and superstars "Amen!"
  And so the Queen – like God, whose power
Was also supervisory –
  Seemed very good. After an hour
She passed us by. Her stringency
  Would turn the milk and honey sour,
And yet we cheer her when she passes –
  Defender of the status quo
From heresy. The cruel sun-glasses
  Of boss or generalissimo,
Beaming upon the obedient masses,
  Windowed her bright black carapace.
But there was never such a God.

And a pale, stubborn, empty face
And white-gloved hand, waving the rod
  We kiss, were all her signs of grace.
– Imagine the chaos and surprise
  If she'd changed her route and quietly come
With interrogation in her eyes
  Into our kitchen, met *our* "Mum",
Had tea and talked of families!
  But not the chaos of an age
Which bred its vulgar Coriolans –
  Beyond free verse and off the stage –
To take the law in their own hands
  And fire whole nations with their rage . . .
Words slip and slide. Which body of thought
  Can flower here uninfected? Who
Now hears the ego writhe where it's caught –
  For the delectation of the few –
Out-of-joint in the verse it wrought?
  The "age demands" role, meaning, style;
Narcissus in the barbed wire fence
  Of past and future will revile
And praise in his own self-defence.
  The window reflects my defensive smile:
Who chooses which lines he'll live along?
  The phones on both sides of the road
Are silent now. Spontaneous song,
  As Friday evening lightens the load
On my mind, would come out tired and wrong.
  So better go and help to put
The kids to bed. The padded world
  Of P's and Q's, "But yes", "Yes but"
Stuns us – like bolts of traffic hurled
  Through patient jams. So go on foot
By sidestreets and across the park
  And be less patient with loud lights,

88

More patient with this dark and that dark,
  Less careless of who wrongs your rights,
More careful of the iron lark
  Whose right- and left-wing engines sing
While we're snowed under here on earth
  (As Heine said) as if the spring
Were theirs to summon. So weigh the worth
  And worthlessness of taking wing. –
Material-minded through and through,
  The takers now have taken over
So thoroughly that any who
  Is still a giver, liver, lover,
Had better be a liar too –
  As Heine was. An honest man,
He might have said, is one who knows
  More or less when he's lying – an
Unhealthy running saw to those
  Whose mores are more puritan.
Flattering, complaining, wangling, he
  Waged life like a one-man guerrilla war
Against a Romantic century:
  Destroyed but undefeated, he bore
A lot of painful poetry,
  Whose purest patterns neither win
Nor lose but grow in each of us.
  But the worst comes to the worst within.
All do what everybody does.
  Are these the wages of our sin?
Why should we feel life always was
  Redeemed by putting up with things?
I'm here because I'm here because
  I pay my bills. My grubby wings
Were formed and clipped by unwritten laws.
  But beyond our scurrying fantasies
Other forms move – of time, of space.

If our oldest stories mould what is,
If the only facts in such a case
    Are feelings, dreams, appearances,
We must re-dream ourselves. Like cars,
    We twinkle loudly through the dusk,
As whiz-kids follow board-room stars –
    And I and others wore subfusc –
And soldiers will embark for wars;
    Though now across this darkened road
I see a tailor's dummy, white
    And blind, lean from a black explod-
ed window. But I hope to write
    Until my mind and life have slowed.

PART FOUR
Interpretations

1. HAMLET IN ENGLAND

"*Polonius: What do you read, my lord?*
Hamlet : Words, words, words.
Polonius: What is the matter, my lord?
Hamlet : Between who?"

In other versions of the legend than Shakespeare's, Hamlet reaches England, whose king (according to his uncle's plan) is to put him to death. But Hamlet rewrites his retainers' letters, requesting that the bearers be executed. The rewritten letters also propose that Hamlet should marry the king of England's daughter. And this marriage takes place. After a year Hamlet returns to Denmark and avenges what he is by now convinced was his father's murder. He explains and justifies himself to the people, who acclaim him king.

In the following version, Hamlet has left the government of the country in the hands of Laertes, with whom he has become reconciled, and has returned with his wife and two-year-old daughter to England.

Still out of joint
My thoughts withdraw
Sometimes for hours
To Elsinore.

The foolish people
And cloud-capped towers
Of that solid castle
Were a prison to me

Whose confines, wards
And dungeons weren't real
But still make me feel
Like some sort of vassal,
Bounded, unfree.

I disappoint
My father-in-law.
The English expect
Action. But I
Too often see
In my mind's eye
The ghosts of that place –

My uncle's face
Like a weathercock

Which ambitious minions
Hoping to flatter
Would timidly inspect
Before daring to utter
Their considered opinions.

Whoever spoke
Would conduct an inspection
Of the wind's direction
Pretty precisely

For fear the old
Bear, Boreas,
Might snort at them
Not very nicely.

In fact the cleverest
Kept quite mum:
A smiling echo
In that court distorted
With malice aforethought
Each word or sigh
Or hopeless cry
That it reported.

Down in the orchard
Where my father died,
Unweeded, grown
To seed, there stood
A fountain, ornamented
With sphinxes, whose stone
Was always dry
Except for when I
Had vented

My feelings. How
I curse that place!
The bitter tears,
The bitterer blood!
And the venomous brood
Of eavesdropping rats
And adders which crept
Into every hide-out
Where I inwardly wept
Or raged and cried out.
I see them now
At my uncle's face,
But they take the forms
Of maggots and worms.

He's dead and gone.
So why these fears
With no real object?
Or am I their subject?
It's two whole years

Since the poison made
Him swell up and cry
And beg to be killed.

I watched him die.
I wasn't afraid
To feel fulfilled.

His life was a blight
On any beauty.
Surely I was right
About my duty?

Down in that garden
Where my father died
He begged my pardon,
But I denied
Him the comfort. Instead,
I didn't care if I sinned:
As he suffered, I grinned
Where I used to squat
And try to hide!
I had howled and cried
In that filthy spot:
I had wished I was dead,
That my flesh would melt
Like a thing of nothing,

Like the nightingale
Who loved to sing
Where the roses rot.

My curse on that garden!
There'd been times when I'd felt
Afraid of ghosts
By day! The light
Itself seemed blighted –
Heavy with curses,
Haunted, benighted,

As though his corpse
Had begun to sprout.

And how weary and stale,
Like the brown fog
Of a winter dawn,
The air had smelt.

The ghost that came,
Although it seemed
A paternal Samson
To my uncle's lecherous
Solomon, harrowed
My heart with fear –

And my mind with doubt:
As if I'd dreamed
Them its words became
Unreal and treacherous,
My guilt in borrowed
Glory. It seemed –

And seems – to me
That with bloated words –
Like "nightmare" or "history" –
And pictures we

(But what have I
To do with you?
Or you with me?)

From inside out

Conceal our sin
From ourselves and from grace:

Unctuous, but blistery,
We film and skin
The ulcerous place

Interpreting words
And pictures which
Interpret words
And pictures which

Interpret "things".

The corruption within
Infects unseen,

And how or why
Things seem to mean
Something – or nothing –
Had better remain

(As it always will,
While words have wings
Of nothing but breath
And pictures are seen
By mortal eyes)

Even to the wise
A mystery . . .

What's realest is death,

From which we flee
By other lies . . .

But who could express
This in words any finer
Than those of Heine? –
Let me see, let me see –
"And then a spookiness . . ."
How does that stanza begin?
Ah, yes. With "Then a green . . .":

Then a green spookiness would grin
At me – seem cruelly to be scoffing –
While out of a squat yew-tree 'd come
A death-like moaning, gasping, coughing.

Escaping down the avenue
To where the terrace rose to meet me,
I'd watch the North Sea's flood-tide waves
Crash on the rocks as if to greet me.

And there you could gaze far out to sea.
Often I stood there wildly dreaming.

The sea of troubles in my breast
Was also foaming, storming, screaming!

The screaming, storming, foaming in
My breast had surged up no less proudly
But had become as powerless as
The waves the rocks smashed up so loudly.

With envious eyes I watched the ships
Sail off to better, happier lands!
But that damned castle held me fast,
Although I cursed its bitter bonds.

And if I'd nursed
His head in my hands,
How much more would I see?
How much more would I know
Objectively?
For all I can tell
Of *it* from *me,*
I might as well
Be a lonely tree
On some barren height,
Benumbed and white
In the mist and snow.

Am I awake
Or do I dream
On my Northern hill?

And how should I make
A decision to go?

Such things only seem,
But the thought returns

To comfort me still
Of a distant palm.
Where do such thoughts
Originate? –
Ought-nots and oughts,
What to love, what to hate? –
Does this palm in the East
Of my mind only mock?

She probably burns
On a wall of rock,
Grieving, alone.

Does she scream, or groan?

What ought I to do?
O my wife, o my daughter,
Was the play the thing?
I wish I knew.
My daughter plays
By the garden swing.
What now of self-slaughter?
"I want it" she says,
And tries to bite
Her picture book.
Her tearful look
Makes neither the fruit
Nor her wish come true.

"That's blue" she says
Of the built-up blocks
Which are red. The row
Of paints in her box
Makes sudden sense. –
At the age of two,

Though the bucket and spade
Which she thinks are blue
Were red before
She said so, who
Can call a shade a shade?

"It's my go now"
She says. But she's pulled
And pushed from the swing. –
If fair is fair
At two years old,
But another's fair
Is another thing,
And your point of view
Gets tumbled and rolled
And sat on, who
Would not run away crying?

She cannot know
How ill all's here
About my heart.

But her laugh is a cry
Which helps me defy
The infected part
Played by the voice
Of guilt or fear.

She weeps like a smile –
And sheds a smile
Like a leaf or a tear!

Will she help me make
A decision to go?
The longer I stay
The weaker I grow.

When sparrows fall,
It's because they fly.

But they're guiltless of choice,
Whereas you and I
Must decide to take

Another breath,
Another way:

O my wife,
O my daughter,
The readiness is all –
For death,
For life.

If it be now
It's not to come.
If it be not
To come, it will
Be now. If it
Be not now, yet
It will come. Let
Be.

2. A BOHEMIAN PAINTER GOES MADDER

i

If You're Right, You're Wrong

The painter doffs his floppy hat
And (discreetly) dons a businessman's.
Why should he look
Like this or like that? –
The geo-physicist's wife along the road,
Doing a doctorate in philosophy, wears
The latest student fashions, believes
In the unification of society.
To explain this she refers
To mythemes, semes and phemes,
Dicent-symbol-legisigns,
Rhematic-indexical-sinsigns and
Icons. The painter
Is racking his mind with hats
Whose conflicting modes of good and bad
Around him and within him
Bedazzle and bedim him
Until his mind's reeling
As if he were drunk or mad.
How do you think colourfully when your soul
Is heady with conflict? Or choose your style
From who can tell how many ways
Of seeing / ways
Of saying? Your role
Is also yours to choose.
The cameras smile.
And though we shan't all miss what we lose

The painter sees his soul crack into bits
And turns in terror from that jangling vision
Where nothing combines or fits
And his feelings contradict his considered opinion
And his opinions and his feelings somehow differ
When the matter concerns himself from when it concerns
His wife, his family, social circle, the political
Set-up in the land he happens to live in,
His religious world, his business world.

ii

If You Win, You Lose

"The camera bares omnivorous teeth:
Its '*seems*' is all we have of '*is*'.
The stranger's head, hidden beneath
Its cast-iron cloth, breeds jealousies.

"I snap my camera back at him:
We pose before each other lest
With crazy intellectual zest
Some keyed-up *Wildschwein* trample the gem

"Which subtle, camera-snouted pigs –
And fat pink prudent slotted ones
With identical specs, false teeth and wigs –
Competing with pearl-handled guns,

"Shoot to protect – the brittle glass
With many, many facets,
Which some have seen on the steel grass,
In shiny, tiny bits."

iii

Visiting the Mad

Ignored by these viewers,
A frustrated would-be ace
  Screws up Wimbledon

                .

Mixed has-beens (horny
And highly-strung as catgut)
  Lick or chew the mike

                .

Flashers and nymphos
Sit slamming lonely foreheads
  In their distant cells

                .

Now in the corner
Some madman's climbing Everest –
  By himself, of course

                .

Vexed by empty shelves,
Poets CRY. For attention.
  By hook or by crook

                .

Is this a mad–house,
Mountain, book–shop, office–block –
  Or run–down brothel

                ?

On, on! In on. Up
On. On up, on up, on up,
   Up, UP! Down. And out

                  .

If we can't get no
Satisfaction, we don't want
   No satisfaction

                  .

Nerves knotted, wired to
The gabbling set, millions lust
   For gold and silver

                  .

Unattainable
Rewards! Even vengeance is
   Unattainable

                  .

You can't win, can you?
But what if you're punished for
   Losing? Here they know

                  .

Break things till a nurse
Straps you howling to a post!
   Smash your own face up.

3. IN LIEU OF A MANIFESTO: HEINE'S GRAVE

"I am only too aware that my position is unnatural: everything
I do is folly to the sensible - and an abomination to the foolish!"
Heine, **Ideas. The Book Of Le Grand**

Angrily crossing the *Place*
    de la Concorde, with the pram
Coming in handy for stopping
    four – five – six lanes of cars,
Poisoning my lungs with their fumes,
    deafening my ears with their din –
Freedom of movement, I thought,
    added a dimension to life! –
We pause at last for a breather
    beside the obelisk where
The guide-book informs us *Madame*
    la Guillotine did her duty
By Louis XVI, Marie-
    Antoinette, Danton, Robespierre,
"Among others" – and try to consider
    how to retreat from this strange
Disease of mechanized life
    up through the streets of Montmartre
Into the silence that grows
    plant-like and motionless where
The named and nameless have lain
    under the yew-trees, famed
Or forgotten, for hundreds of years.

    "Heinrich Heine" – it's here.
White now. A lyre and a bust

have rendered it poetical – too
Much of a monument. Still,
    somebody's put a few flowers
At the foot of his pedestal, fresh
    primroses stuck in a jar
Filled by the rain to the brim.
    Easter is early this year:
Coldly, sadly the rain
    drips from leafless limetrees
Onto the jumble of graves.
    Far from home, in Montmartre,
Heine lies, who foresaw
    better than Marx, and more fully
Than any English Romantic,
    our 'modern' world and its art.

Rightly he feared us! Although
    communists no longer, we
Guilt-ridden, gloomy iconoclasts
    of sublimity, Beauty and Truth,
Have chopped down his laurels and planted
    potatoes – trampled the pale
And idle lilies, the indolent
    roses, for failing to make
A material contribution
    to the good of society. And,
As for his nightingales, most
    of our vulgar generation
Would hardly know if we'd heard one
    singing its "plaintive anthem" –
Or care very much if we had.
    Afraid that his poor *Book of Songs*
Would be turned into paper bags
    for grocers to fill with their coffee
And snuff for the hags of the future,

still he felt bound to accept
That, if the premise was true
   that all have the right to eat,
The world and his art must suffer
   the consequences. Foreseeing
The worst of these consequences,
   with the demons of logic dancing
About him in triumph, Heine,
   in danger of losing his wits –
Snatching the wreath from his brow –
   awaiting the fall of the king –
Nevertheless cried out,
   "Let justice be done! Our world
Has been weighed in the balance and found
   wanting! And blessed be the grocer
Who turns my books into bags
   for the coffee, potatoes and snuff
Of the ancient women who now
   go gathering fuel to survive
The comfortless winter. *Fiat*
   justitia, pereat mundus!"

Communists no longer – nor fascists
   or anti-Semites (though who
Can honestly say that he
   has never been either? Not
The best – or the most creative –
   among us!) – since neither left
Nor right is the thing to be
   at this critical moment in time –
We, the politically correct,
   have all been to college, and learned
To do things in order. Our grandparents
   succeeded in selling the grocers
Quite so much produce (potatoes

included) – in driving such bargains
For the powers and ductile skills
   of their minds and bodies – *or* Mammon,
The glittering god, intervened
   in his usual mysterious way
To perform a *Wirtschaftswunder*
   on their needy behalf – that now
We who were once the lumpen
   poor have got enough money
To purchase our produce back,
   or to pay for an education
In order to have a career
   as middle-class lawyers or teachers –
Executives, hairdressers, artists –
   or to go on expensive holidays
Abroad. And the grocers created
   quite so much wealth by selling
Coffee, potatoes and snuff
   to the formerly poor and the rich –
Soapsuds, alcohol, books –
   TVs, cameras, cars –
Electronic commun-
   -ication gadgets and fads –
Constantly changing fashions
   in clothing, music, bikes –
And other such stuff without which
   life has become intolerable –
Or Mammon the omnipotent god
   intervened on their greedy behalf –
That now they've become the richest
   ladies and lords of Philistia,
Seizing the levers of legal –
   political – monetary power.

"Wo wird einst des Wandermüden
   Letzte Ruhestätte sein?"

Has, since Arnold was here,
  been chiselled on Heine's grave.
And yet for two hundred years
  we poets have loudly and proudly
Proclaimed that our books are not paper
  bags of any description
While slowly, unsurely, retreating –
  some inwardly, others withdrawing
Physically – from here and now:
  to lakesides, meadows and hills –
Oneness with nature – with lovers –
  daydreams, the free creative
Imagination, *Sehnsucht*
  for the simple, solitary realm
Where the noble Savage ran
  As free as Nature first made man,
Ere Servitude began;
  to the manna and milk of Paradise –
Where all should cry *Beware*
  his flashing eyes! his hair! –
Retreating from money's rant,
  withdrawing from lack of interest
To visions of unacknowledged
  yet potent legislation;
Turning from turning backs
  to myopic élitism – arrogant
Allusive / elusive obscurity –
  political resignation –
Art for art's sake, bardolatry –
  art for *my* sake, self-worship –
The egotistical sublime
  disappearing up its own arsehole,
Mistaking marbles for marvels,
  melodious mouthings for meaning –
Arcane and ancient religions,

inflating egoless egos –
All-knowing, smart-remarking
   intellectual self-assertion,
Driving out *angst* with hubris,
   chagrin with the salve of renown –
Erhebung of normalcy, the female
   demotic *(She crooks the bottle:*
How her daughter suckles!) –
   hubris beating down hubris
From high Romanticism
   to low Romanticism,
Disassembling formal constraints,
   dismantling 'poetic' personae –
Fantasies, megalomania –
   infantilism, melancholy, booze –
Solipsistic reflections,
   the odd-bod's bog of self-pity –
The affected indifference or toughness
   of unimportant outsiders –
Badness, gladness, madness –
   suicide, premature death:
To obscure and gloomy hide-outs,
   crowded with memories of home,
Ecstatic or frightened children –
   (this childish generation! –
Spoiled and petulant, softly
   shifting the blame onto life) –
Parents reminded of innocence,
   admiring themselves in their children,
Reminded of what they've lost:
   to ranches of isolation,
Suburbs to believe and die in,
   valleys which no executive
Would be silly enough to enter
   or stupid enough to foreclose.

A sorry, dishonest spectacle –
    interrupted, it's true,
By brilliant and sometimes brave –
    or self-destructive – engagement,
Over against the humdrum,
    with whatever's doing the damage
To however we choose to pass
    our time in this iron time
Of doubts, disputes, distractions,
    benumbing our souls, as in winter –
But, to our shame, primarily
    bossed by bullies and loud-mouths,
Turning poetry into
    an ethereal / material commodity –
By cultural aristocrats who
    sell their gifts discreetly –
Sciolists, pseuds and ruthless
    sons-of-bitches – half-barmy
Bards of suburban Bohemia –
    drug-users, drop-outs, drunks;
As well as by those who, unable
    to outdo the masses, have joined them –
Performers and entertainers –
    play-actors, singers, dancers,
And even striptease artists –
    jokers, smart-alecs, hard-knocks,
Blowing their own brass trumpets –
    politic publishers – po-biz
Organizers and judges –
    Grub-street politics – pushy
Journalists posing as editors,
    editors posing as critics,
Critics posing as poets,
    grinding aesthetical axes,
Making it *new* – 'New Gen' –

'New Formalism' – new
Trend-setting in-crowds, seeking
    media attention, turning
Poetry into a variety
    of middle-brow song and dance.

"Wo wird einst des Wandermüden
Letzte Ruhestätte sein?"

  Where?

Sick and tired of life's long journey,
Where at last will I recline?
Under mezzogiorno palmtrees?
Under limetrees on the Rhine?

Will I lie in some strange desert,
Buried by an unknown hand?
Or may I, beside the ocean,
R.I.P. in coastal sand?

Anyway! God's sky-blue heaven
Will surround me, here or there,
And at night the stars, like death-lamps,
Will attend me anywhere.

And while I mused night swiftly ran
Across the cloudy sky;
The wind tore at the trees: it began
To rain. And suddenly

A familiar disembodied voice
Was in my ear. It said,
"Poor Arnold really had no choice –
Even though his dad was dead –

"But to tut-tut my one-off sort
Of reckless wit. Sincerely
Fearing to say what he really thought –
Or even to think it clearly –

"Afraid to watch and wait alone,
Or slip the feeble chain
Of such as bluster, cringe and groan
Across the hectic plain

"Of 'modern life', he ran with those
Who led the dreary slog,
Policing the herd, keeping them close
Together, like a dog.

"But though he did his dogged duty
By the holy cow of Culture,
The half-gone god of Truth and Beauty
Was torn by the big-beaked vulture

"On John Bull's wrist. The Philistines,
As in his heart he knew,
Had long since won. They drew the lines
Round all he'd ever do.

"At all the *sides in man* he aimed
And emptily discussed them
Within a conscience bound and maimed
By his mighty father, Rustum.

" 'But was it thou – I think', he claimed,
'Surely it was! – that bard
Whom Goethe' – leaving names unnamed –
'Found gifted but loveless and hard?

" 'Love, without which even the tongues
Of angels sound amiss!'
The age demanded love in its songs –
And bared its bum to kiss.

"Such wet-legs with such infant's needs
The powers-that-be found *Great
And Good*. Such 'love' as theirs concedes
The game to greed and hate:

"A compromise, an abdication
Of responsibility,
An (ig)noble-minded (im)moral evasion
Of whatever it means to be free!

"The child is father of the man –
But a lot of skewed behaviour
Can come from viewing Peter Pan
As mankind's latest saviour.

"Innocence fades. It cannot last,
Nor should it. Live here now,
Not in some happy / unhappy past
Or wished-for future *'Wow!'*:

" 'In the huge world which roars hard by
Be others happy if they can!
But in my helpless cradle I
Was breathed on by the rural Pan.'

"His life and poetry never came
Together. Copping out,
He got a job and married. Tamed,
He burbled on about

" 'The harmony from which man swerved
Made his life's rule once more!
The universal order served!
Earth happier than before!'

"In the huge world which roared hard by
He sought and found respect,
And gave up writing poetry
While there were schools to inspect.

"He thought the schools would help each boy
And girl to strive to attain
'One common wave of thought and joy
Lifting mankind again!'

"Whereas all 'common thought' still finds
The poet's life pure folly.
And modern fools have gone quite blind
Grubbing for love or lolly.

"The 'universal order' now
Is grab it while you can,
And all the ancient gods shall bow
To democratic man.

"Nor is there any other way,
Since people must be fed.
Some evils now have had their day.
But others have raised their head.

   "In the words of a fellow–exile:
'Such is the structure of life
    that what we regard as Evil
Can develop into a fairly
    ubiquitous presence, if only

Because it tends to appear
   in the guise of good. You never
See it crossing the threshold
   announcing "Hi, I'm Evil!"

" 'The surest defence against Evil
   is extreme individualism . . .
Something that cannot be feigned
   or faked or imitated,
Something even a seasoned
   impostor couldn't be happy with:
Something, in other words,
   that can't be shared – like your skin –
Not even by a minority.
   Evil's a sucker for solidity:
It always goes for big numbers . . .'

"I thought I'd knick-knacks in my books –
'Jewels to crown and enthrone one' –
But now, I must admit, it looks
As if the great Unknown One

"Has fallen to the Golden Calf
Or, at the very least,
To a bread-and-butter image of
Some less than happy beast!

"Don't worry, I won't quote again
From foreign fields. But, you see,
You English were such gentlemen
In the 19th century,

"Such patriotic monarchists,
Such soulful Darwinian lords,
Such teachers, such coarse optimists,
Such dopes, such pious frauds,

"How *could* you think – locked in the box
The age had set you in –
Or see beyond it? But the locks
Were only made of sin.

"In Germany I quickly learned
Never to trust the poetical.
In earlier times they might have burned
Me and my books as heretical.

"The poet's business is to tell
The truth as far as he
Can see or say it. The victim's yell
Of agony or glee,

"His loves, his hates, his lifelong struggle
To join the crowd, or beat it –
His angry pride – or Arnoldian haggle
To have his cake and eat it –

"His self-assertive song and dance,
His shifting of the blame
To God or Mum-and-Dad or chance,
Though at first they look the same,

"Appear as passive in the test
Of time, which also tells
The truth. For truth is active. Best
Re-dream your heavens, your hells . . .

"And yet I soon became too ill
To pursue with zeal or zest
The holy grail of man's free will,
Which might have been my quest . . .

"What Brodsky meant was *Wield your wit*
To fight a peaceful war,
Which is the very opposite
Of bawling 'I (won't) withdraw!'

"I understood that neither attack
Nor retreat could in the end
Release me from the turning back
Of enemy or friend –

"That cries of neither *Us and Them*
Nor *All for One* . . . are free;
That all such slogans also stem
From locks we cannot see –

"And if our world's a gaol of lies,
Or a huge and evil derangement,
Perhaps the greatest freedom lies
In unembittered estrangement . . .

"But I too got lost in that dark age
Of sick fatigue and doubt.
And all my flights of spite or rage
Could never fly me out.

"And so, for myself, I wish
    they'd left me the tombstone that Arnold –
I remember him well, poor Sohrab,
    I remember his mutton-chop whiskers –
Recoiled from in fear and self-pity:
    ' "*Henri Heine*" – 'tis here!
That black tombstone, the name
    carved there – no more!' No dates,
No epitaph, and no poem:
    that which is nameless may not

Be named, after all – a source
    of comfort and joy to me,
Though of melancholy to Matthew.
    At the end of my days, with *la Mouche* –
The sweet little fly who sang
    about my decaying body –
I was perfectly happy. Well,
    enough of that. I suppose
Some verses there'll have to be.
    So may I express a preference?" –

Jetzt Wohin?

Where to now? My brainless feet
Turn towards the German border.
Common sense, though, shakes its head –
Sets my muddled thoughts in order:

Yes, the war is over now,
But the war-trials are indicting
Such as you, who once, it seems,
Penned some punishable writing.

Well, it's true, a firing squad
Seems a nasty way to snuff it.
And I lack the tragic mien
Which might show them where to stuff it.

– O to be in England! *But*
All those sweaty English faces,
Steam and coal-smoke, sicken me,
Causing cramps in several places.

Sometimes I believe I'll sail
Off to Freedom's mighty stable

In the USA, where hicks
Fraternize at any table.

But it worries me that they
Chew tobacco, play at skittles
With no king of any sort
Or spittoon to catch their spittles.

Russia's splendid empire might
Please me better. And I'd dare it,
But the knout in winter, well,
I don't think that I could bear it.

Sadly I inspect the sky
Where a thousand stars are dozing.
But among so many I
Cannot see my own reposing.

Lost perhaps. Astray in heaven's
Labyrinthine golden mystery.
Just as I have gone astray
In the sludge of human history.

4. PICASSO'S CHILDREN.
OR: WAYS OF SEEING / WAYS OF SAYING

"Probably I don't have a style. As often as not, style is something
that ties an artist down to the same way of seeing, to the same
technique, the same formulations . . . You recognize it at once, but
it's always the same suit of clothes . . . As for myself, I hit out too
wildly, am too much of a vagabond. You see me here but already
I've changed and am somewhere else. I'm never tied down. That's
why I don't have a style."

Picasso

1895-1897
A barefoot girl, wearing a plain red dress,
Plays queen on a barren patch of dusty ground.
Behind her the dark and threatening emptiness
Could panic her soft eyes with one big bound.

And so a feverish woman lies in bed
Nursed by an elderly doctor and young nun,
Who holds her child. Yet when her mother's dead
This child – and then her children – will live on

In unassertive innocent affirmation,
Like Pablo's sister kneeling all in white
At First Communion. Her parents' resignation
Highlights her pureness. But in the timeless light

She cannot know and they're too old to learn
Two candles dead means two are left to burn.

1901

After Picasso's impotent friend
Had blown out his brains,
                              the heartless spring
Arrived with its usual flurry and fling
Of seed and sunshine.
                              A bitter end,
But artists / children keep repeating
The old made new.
                              A girl with a bowl
Concentrates heart and guts and soul
On what she stands at the table eating.

Another cuddles a dove.
                              She sends
A sweet demanding look of the sort
No well-trained parent would wish to refuse.
But though she performs
                              and the other blends
Into the background, lost in thought,

How freely do children / artists choose?

1902-1906

Clasping her thin blue child, a mother waits
On a dismal shore for an ominous empty boat
To fetch them. The child absorbs her sickly whites
But not the tiny red of the flower she's brought.
And even the family of tumblers, left behind
Or waiting, oppress the children, like the thumb
And little finger of a hopeless hand
Raised in the wasteland. But who oppresses *them?*
Across that dusty ground a short time after
A naked boy comes leading a bright grey horse:
At home, the departed tumblers' drum becomes

A table, while their daughter's abandoned flowers
Blush in a vase. And his pick-a-backed brother's laughter
Helps free his growing body's grace and force.

1923-1924 / 1954

*"Now, Kitty," said Alice, "let's consider who it was
that dreamed it all."*

To the upside-down world it was Pablo who said
"I've a harlequin-suit on, and eyes in my head:
Let all back-to-front creatures, whoever they be,
Come and pose for Queen Olga, Pablito and me."

"Come take up your cameras as quick as you can
Before he becomes a wild Minotaur man –
Or changes his mind or his clothes or his wife!
And let's all wish King Pablo a very long life!"

"O arse-licking crawlers," said Pablo, "draw near:
It's an honour to meet you, a favour to hear!
Your creeping-and-crawling 's a pleasure to see
For Claude and Paloma, Queen Françoise and me."

*

And as children make-believe their roles are real,

> He'd substitute
> For "harlequin-suit"

> *Gentleman's wig –*
> *Blue Period coat –*

Bright red cravat
(Absurdly big) –
Catalan hat –

Braque's uniform –
Prize-fighter's shorts –
Sporran and kilt
(Absurdly warm) –
Etc. –

To fit the ways we see and think and feel.

1934-1937
Guided towards his Apollonian self
By a girl he trusts, who cuddles a soft white dove,
The Minotaur heaves his huge blind heavy head
To the starry sky in search of innocent love.

And now he's in danger. A screaming, flailing horse
Could stamp him to death.
                        Unless the living light
Of the girl's small candle leads him to a ladder
And both escape
                to watch the final fight
Of bull and mare
                from the dove-cote above.

But the child is dead and the bull alive and kicking
Under an eye-bulb sun.
                        When a Nazi asked him
"Did you do that?"
                        Picasso said, "No, you did."
And long before the artist
                        history chose

No language but the cry

                       of children afraid of the night

Because they have not been good.

1656 / 1957
(Self-Portrait as a Gentleman-In-Waiting)

Trying to believe

            he's bigger than

                      the maids-

And ladies-in-waiting,

                the Infanta Margarita Maria

And the docile dog being kicked by an attendant midget,

The thin blue painter,

              holding his palette and brushes,

Only succeeds in looking unsure of himself,

As though in his heart of hearts

                  he wished he could blend –

As he seems to do –

           into the blues of the background.

His studio imprisons him.

                Are the hooks in the ceiling

For lights?

        His subjects – the King and Queen –

Are only seen

          in a mirror

              on the far wall

                  behind him,

So that he and the children look

              in our direction.

And I ask
        myself:
                Are artists still nothing but minions,
Like such gentlemen-in-waiting
                        long ago –
Or

is	who
it	see
only	them
I	so?

1973 – 1999 –

Children were not a danger. Being a child
In so many ways himself, he never snarled
At them again. Or cubed them into cold
And distant forms. Instead, while they revealed

A fresh new way of looking, he painted and lolled
In their mothers' and others' arms. Playful, self-willed,
When life as moulded by each body dulled
He left and began again, re-making the world

From a fresh new model, aesthetically impelled
To demonstrate the ways in which he ruled
The space between ourselves and the endless, unspoiled
Flux of what really happens. It never failed

For him. But abandoned mothers and children sprawled
To bitter ends. Art was his only child.

Acknowledgements
AND NOTES

Sections and passages from *Then And Now* first appeared in the following magazines: *Acumen, Bare Bones, The Dark Horse, Haiku Quarterly, Iota, Iron, Leviathan Quarterly, Modern Poetry In Translation, Oasis, Orbis, Outposts, Pennine Platform, Stand, The Rialto*.

An extract from *From Hand To Mouth* was published under the title *Snowed Under* in the Arvon Poetry Competition 1987 Anthology. "Words, words, words, and nothing doing!" was recorded by the author for the *Literaturtelefon*, Munich.

The poems and translations were written between 1981 and 1999, and revised in 2001. English titles for the translations from Heine are listed in the Contents.

p.15 **"this strange disease of modern life"**: As long ago as 1853 Matthew Arnold wrote in *The Scholar Gipsy*:

> O born in days when wits were fresh and clear,
>   And life ran gaily as the sparkling Thames;
>   Before this strange disease of modern life
> With its sick hurry, its divided aims,
>   Its heads o'ertaxed, its palsied hearts, was rife –
>   Fly hence, our contact fear! . . .

Not that flight – or any other form of Romantic withdrawal – has been of much help . . . Arnold makes a fuller appearance below in *In Lieu Of A Manifesto: Heine's Grave*, while the Scholar Gipsy turns up in the alternative (or concomitant) Romantic mode of self-assertion as Eliot's Coriolan (see *Difficulties Of A White-Collar Worker*) – still "waiting for the spark from Heaven to fall", in Arnold's beautiful but useless words . . .

p.18 *Difficulties of a White-Collar Worker:* Cf. T.S. Eliot, *Coriolan* (1931). The poem presumes that the "young Cyril" mentioned in *Triumphal March* is the son of "Arthur Edward Cyril Parker". Shortly before writing *Coriolan*, T.S.E. formulated his well-known description of his "general point of view . . . as classicist in literature, royalist in politics and anglo-catholic in religion" (*For Lancelot Andrewes*, 1928). In 'The Function Of Criticism' (1923) Eliot had characterized – or rather, caricatured – the difference between Classicism and Romanticism as "the difference between the complete and the fragmentary, the adult and the immature, the orderly and the chaotic". Probably not even his worst enemy would want to describe Old Possum's poetry as fragmentary, immature and chaotic. Even so, it is now difficult to understand how anyone could have been taken in by his claim to be a "classicist in literature". On the other hand, as Peter Ackroyd points out, "Almost from the beginning Eliot had a clear understanding of the mechanics of making a literary reputation . . ." (*T.S. Eliot*, 1984, p.101).

The sequence also alludes to *The Waste Land* and other works by Eliot.

p.21 *Heinrich Heine: Deutschland. Ein Wintermärchen:* Heine wrote this poem – which is over 2000 lines in length – in about six weeks at the beginning of 1844 after spending two months in his native Germany. He had moved to Paris in 1831, inspired by the July Revolution which deposed Charles X, the last Bourbon king, and placed the citizen-king Louis-Philippe on the throne. In the meantime Heine's reputation as a radical had been sufficient for the German authorities to ban his writings and while in Germany he was in some danger of being arrested. Apart from another trip to Germany later in 1844, Heine was to spend the remainder of his life in Paris, where he died in 1856.

p.23 **Jandl,** *Aus der Fremde:* Ernst Jandl (1925-2000) was a leading Viennese poet – a self-confessed pessimist with a fine sense of black humour. Sub-sections *ii, v, xiv, xviii* and *xix* of *From Hand To Mouth* are adapted from his work. His 'speech-opera' *Aus der Fremde* is, among other things, a portrait of himself attempting to write the very play in which he is the principal character. The dialogue takes place entirely in the third person and in a form of reported speech which can be used to imply hypothesis or unreality. This makes the play practically untranslatable since this form has no reliable equivalent in English. The epigraph, roughly translated, means:

> *(He:)* *whether the broken half*
> *always had to fall*
> *with the jam-side down*
>
> *ever disgustedly*
> *did he make use of*
> *the little hand-brush*
>
> *trivialities of that kind*
> *kept jolting into*
> *his very existence!*

p.29 **Hoffmann von F.**: Hoffmann von Fallersleben (1798-1874), a popular poet "dismissed from his Breslau professorship in 1842 for his ironically titled *Unpolitical Songs* . . . He became for a while the beatnik poet of nineteenth-century Germany, travelling from tavern to tavern with his guitar and simple and humorous but biting songs . . . [Heine] came to abominate [him]; he took Hoffmann as a symptom of the destruction of poesy by democracy, a process in which he considered political poetry to be a transitional phenomenon . . ." (J.L. Sammons, *Heinrich Heine: A Modern Biography*, 1979, p.255).

With regard to the translations and quotations in the sequence as a whole, Jorge Luis Borges, for example, in 'Pierre Menard, Author of the Quixote', has demonstrated – among other things – the infinite applications of "deliberate anachronism and erroneous attribution . . ." In the sequence-within-the-sequence the translations are, obviously, an aspect of the 'Self-Portrait As . . .' Acknowledging Eliot as his precursor, Borges also observes that "Every writer creates his own precursors. His work modifies our conception of the past, as it will modify the future". His example in this case is Kafka, but the arguments in both texts (one fictional, one an essay), as well as in others in *Labyrinths* (1964), are basically elaborations of Borges' conviction that "a book is more than a verbal structure or series of verbal structures; it is the dialogue it establishes with its reader . . . This dialogue is infinite . . . A book is not an isolated being: it is a relationship, an axis of innumerable relationships".

p.52 **I was the man / Who lay there dead**: For the last eight years of his life (from 1848 to 1856) Heine was painfully and increasingly paralysed by a disease of the spinal cord which confined him to what he referred to as his "mattress-grave". The pain was relieved by dripping morphine into wounds kept open for this purpose on his back, but he suffered badly from cramps, bed-sores and sleeplessness as well as from the ravages of his illness. He was also chronically short of money, having lived for virtually his entire working life from his writings. And yet by common consent Heine composed some of his finest poetry during this period. He was looked after by his devoted but almost illiterate French wife, Mathilde. Shortly before the end, however, he fell in love with a mysterious young visitor, whom he nicknamed *"die Mouche"* (the fly). *"Es träumte mir von einer Sommernacht"* is sometimes known as *Für die Mouche*. *"Worte! Worte! keine Taten!"* (p.56) was also addressed to her.

p.58 *"Doubt thou the stars are fire etc."*: The poem presumes (*pace* the Arden *Hamlet*, 1982) that Hamlet knew very well that it was now doubtful whether the sun moved – and was therefore fully aware of the ironies with which his letter to Ophelia is fraught.

p.59 **"The new Philosophy calls all in doubt . . ."**: Donne's poem, *An Anatomie of the World – The First Anniversary* (1611), is mentioned in a related context by Borges in 'The Fearful Sphere of Pascal', in which he offers a somewhat different account of "that dispirited century", the 17th: "the absolute space which had meant liberation to Bruno became a labyrinth and an abyss to Pascal . . . He felt the incessant weight of the physical world . . ." According to Borges, " . . . men felt lost in time and space. In time, because if the future and the past are infinite, there cannot really be a when; in space, because if every being is equidistant from the infinite and infinitesimal, neither can there be a where." He might have added that men must have felt even more lost whenever they, like Pascal – e.g. *Pensées* 68 (ed. Lafuma) – attempted to relate the old idea of God's omniscient omnipotence to the new universe. As long as there was such a God, in other words, the events which ruled our lives were "fearful" indeed. No wonder, then, that Pascal "experienced vertigo, fright and solitude". Or that "he compared our life with that of castaways on a desert island . . ." As for the question of proof, with which Pascal – a mathematician, scientist and technologist – was as obsessed as anyone, *Pensées* 521 observes:

It may be that there are such things as true proofs, but it is not certain.

Thus this only proves that it is not certain that everything is uncertain. To the greater glory of scepticism.

O brave new world!

p.60 **Now that our world has been relieved /... Of nicely explained religion**: In contrast with Borges' attempt to sketch a chapter – as he puts it himself – of "universal history", Eliot misleadingly argues in 'The *Pensées* of Blaise Pascal' (1931) that "although Pascal brings to his work the same powers which he exerted in science, it is not as a scientist that he presents himself". Published in the same year as *Coriolan*, Eliot's essay presents an account of Pascal characteristically limited by its author's unwillingness (or inability) to view Christianity historically and by his outdated and conservative persona (than which nothing could be more different from Borges' "deliberate anachronism") of Christian apologist. The essay is practically an anglo-catholic (and Anglo-American) sermon, in other words, and exhibits Eliot's personal solution of how to assert oneself as a poet/outsider at its most exclusive and least attractive. Fortunately, he did not often apply this particular form of self-inflation to his poetry, although a more cheerful, tougher-minded and more radical individualist than himself – Joseph Brodsky – has written that "If a century can be compared to a political system, a significant portion of this one's cultural climate could well qualify as a tyranny: that of modernism. Or, to put it more accurately, of what sailed under that pennant . . . Had T.S. Eliot, for instance, at the time he read Laforgue, read Thomas Hardy instead . . . , the history of poetry in English this century, or to say the least its present, might be somewhat more absorbing" ('Wooing the Inanimate' in *On Grief and Reason*). However, for Eliot to have embraced Hardy – or, as it does not suit Brodsky's self-confessed polemic to mention, Hardy Eliot – would have required more than exposure to formal influence: it would have required a change of paradigm.

p.76 **These crossed-out lines of Keats'**: The quotation is from a passage in *The Fall of Hyperion* which, although it is included in most modern editions, Keats seems to have cancelled. This cancellation may well have reflected some temporary indecision on the ailing Keats' part as to whether poetry is of any value or use whatever in the modern world: is it not all mere "dreaming", as the passage preceding the cancellation seems to imply . . . ?

p.83 **But its creator / Knew it might save the world**: Cf. Joseph Brodsky: "Now, the purpose of evolution is the survival neither of the fittest nor of the defeatist . . . The purpose of evolution, believe it or not, is beauty, which survives it all and generates truth simply by being a fusion of the mental and the sensual" ('An Immodest Proposal' in *On Grief and Reason*). On the other hand, "There are few cures for hereditary disorders (undetectable, perhaps, in an individual, but striking in a crowd), and what I'm suggesting here is not one of them . . . The fact that we are alive does not mean that we are not sick" (*ibid.*).

p.89 **(As Heine said)**: In his poem *To Georg Herwegh:*

Herwegh, you iron lark!
Like a jubilant bird on the wing,
In holy sunlight you've vanished!
Is Winter really banished?
Is Germany decked with the blossoms of Spring?

Herwegh, you iron lark!
So high through the sky you fling
You quite lose sight of earthly curses:
Only in your verses
Lives the Spring of which you sing.

Georg Herwegh (1817-1875) was a militant radical as well as a poet. Heine regarded simple-minded socialism with almost as much mistrust as German nationalism and wrote this poem, which he handed to Herwegh personally, after the popular success of the latter's *Gedichte eines Lebendigen* (*Poems of a Living Man*) in 1841.

p.93 **But I / Too often see / In my mind's eye** etc.: Cf. "*Es kommt mir nimmer aus dem Sinne*" etc. in Heine's poem *Affrontenburg* (available with a literal prose translation in Peter Branscombe's Penguin selection). In the process of freeing himself from his own as well as the age's Romanticism Heine devoted a good deal of creative energy to investigating and questioning the nature of imagination and of belief. In this respect, as well as in others, he is a Hamlet-like figure and the Hamlet of this poem (who also, of course, quotes from *Hamlet*) adapts and quotes from *Affrontenburg* and another well-known poem of this sort, *Ein Fichtenbaum steht einsam* (also in Branscombe). "Affrontenburg" was the name which Heine gave to the country seat at Ottensen, near Hamburg, of his immensely rich uncle Salomon. Heine, who was short of money for most of his life, had spent much time at "Affrontenburg", and had even fallen in love with his uncle's daughter. The story has often been told (e.g. by J.L. Sammons, *op.cit.*, pp.48-50) of how Uncle Salomon ruthlessly and systematically ruined his own brother Samson, Heine's father, thereby hastening Samson's death. In 1827 Salomon financed a trip to England but Heine found the English a prosaic and conservative people – "disagreeable robots, machines whose internal mainspring is egotism" and whose life and character seemed pervaded by the commercial spirit he abhorred. Nevertheless, he addressed a number of poems to a certain "Kitty Clairmont", who must have pleased him somewhat better . . .

p.107 *In Lieu Of A Manifesto: Heine's Grave:* The third paragraph of this poem consists largely of an adaptation of a famous passage from Heine's preface to *Lutèce* (1855). The poem also quotes from Joseph Brodsky's 'A Commencement

Address' (in *Less Than One*) and Matthew Arnold's poems *Heine's Grave, Lines Written In Kensington Gardens, Memorial Verses* and *Obermann Once More.* In spite of his admiration for Heine's "intense modernism, his absolute freedom, his utter rejection of stock classicism and stock romanticism", and in spite as well of his awareness that in comparison the works of the English Romantics "have this defect: they do not belong to that which is the main current of the literature of modern epochs, they do not apply modern ideas to life", Arnold concluded: "He died and has left a blemished name; with his crying faults – his intemperate susceptibility, his unscrupulousness in passion, his inconceivable attacks on his enemies, his still more inconceivable attacks on his friends, his want of generosity, his sensuality, his incessant mocking – how could it be otherwise? Not only was he not one of Mr Carlyle's 'respectable' people, he was profoundly *dis*respectable; and not even the merit of not being a Philistine can make up for a man's being that . . . Heine had all the culture of Germany; in his head fermented all the ideas of modern Europe. And what have we got from Heine? A half-result, for want of moral balance, and of nobleness of soul and character" (*Essays In Criticism*).

p.108 **better than Marx**: Heine became friendly with Karl Marx in 1844 while the latter was living in Paris. There is a well-known story, which may or may not be apocryphal, that Heine was one day visiting the Marxes when their daughter Jenny began to choke. In the ensuing panic it was Heine who saved the child's life by turning her upside down and slapping her back until the morsel of food was dislodged. He later recommended that Marx should spend more time reading the Bible.

p.116 **He got a job and married**: In 1851 Arnold was appointed to an inspectorship of schools, a post which enabled him to marry and which he held for thirty-five years. Most of his best-known poetry had been written before this time. Heine, on other hand, tended to align himself with society's outcasts and outsiders. In his youth he might have become a banker but displayed little interest and less talent – even with the backing of Uncle Salomon, one of the richest bankers in Hamburg. He then laboriously studied law – at the universities of Bonn, Göttingen and Berlin. Unlike Arnold, who became Professor of Poetry at Oxford, Heine had little time for 19th-century academicism. One of his better-known snubs (quoted by Arnold in *Essays In Criticism*) was to point out that a dreadful fate had been suffered by all three of Napoleon's greatest opponents: Castlereagh had cut his own throat, Louis XVIII had rotted upon his throne – and Professor Saalfeld was still a professor at Göttingen! Elsewhere (in *Die Heimkehr* LVIII) he wrote:

> *This world and this life are just too fragmented:*
> *I'm off to the German Prof. who's invented*
> *A system for putting them back together*
> *That's as clear as beer. With nothing worse*
> *Than his nightgown and other bedroom clobber*
> *He's stopped up the gaps in the universe.*

Even so, in 1825 Heine graduated as a doctor of law. But he never made use of his degree, preferring to live as best he could by his writing.

p 119 In earlier times they might have burned / Me and my books: Or, for that matter, in later times. Heine was born into a Jewish family, converting to Lutheranism in 1825. His conversion was largely for practical reasons, however, and he wrote much prose and many poems on Jewish themes. Heine's feelings with regard to the history and practice of Judaism were ambivalent and far from simple, but he expresses them with characteristic intelligence, delicacy and wit – as in the beautiful *Jehuda ben Halevy*, in which he identifies with the Jewish poets of medieval Spain, presenting them, and also himself (in what has been called "a complex act of self-affirmation"), as typical members of "the House of Schlemiel . . ."

p.123 **Two candles dead** etc.: John Richardson (in *A Life of Picasso*, 1991) drew attention to the fact that, if local records are correct, Picasso had a younger brother (named José, after his father) who must have died in infancy. Picasso's beloved younger sister, Conchita, also died – at the age of seven, only a year before the First Communion of his surviving sister was painted at his father's instigation. Richardson also draws attention to how two of the candles on the altar in this picture are lit and two have gone out: "The candles could . . . stand for the two living and the two dead children. Combined with the rose-petals, emblems of mortality, that are scattered on the altar steps, this device would suggest that this First Communion is also a *memento mori* that could commemorate the dead Conchita as well as the living Lola."

p.125 **To the upside-down world**: Cf. the song ("To the Looking-Glass world it was Alice who said") in *Through The Looking-Glass*, Ch.9. Carroll was a Borgesian "precursor" of Picasso in at least one other respect as well. His Eg(g)ocentricity, Humpty Dumpty – he who takes the logically acceptable but uncommunicative view that "When I use a word, it means just what I choose it to mean – neither more nor less" – also advises Alice to try and look a little different:

"Your face is the same as everybody has – the two eyes, so –" (marking their places in the air with his thumb) "nose in the middle, mouth under. It's always the same. Now if you had the two eyes on the same side of the nose, for instance – or the mouth at the top – that would be some help."

"It wouldn't look nice," Alice objected. But Humpty Dumpty only shut his eyes, and said "Wait till you've tried."

But Alice has no intention of trying – any more than she has of following his example in the use of words:

"The question is," said Alice, "whether you can make words mean so many different things."

To which Humpty replies at his most Picassian: "The question is . . . which is to be master – that's all."

p.125 *Gentleman's wig etc.*: Referring to various self-portraits and photographs of Picasso, who was notoriously fond of dressing up, especially for guests.

p.127 *1656 / 1957:* The subject of this sonnet is the first of Picasso's adaptations of Velasquez' *Las Meninas*, painted in August 1957.

p.128 *1973 – 1999 –* : Picasso died in 1973.